STAY AWAY
from
OPTION D
...and you will be a perfEct parent!

STAY AWAY
from
OPTION *D*
...and you will be a perfEct parent!

A simple philosophy for parenting.
A simple philosophy for life.

Michelle Gambs, MA, LMHC

Grayboy Press
Indianapolis, Indiana

Stay Away From Option D
...and you will be a perfEct parent!
A simple philosophy for parenting.
A simple philosophy for life.

Michelle Gambs

ISBN-13: 978-1-7359953-0-4
Library of Congress Preassigned Control Number (PCN):
2020920242

Grayboy Press
Indianapolis, Indiana

Editor: Janet Schwind
Designer: Suzanne Parada

DEDICATION

To C and G...
A love beyond all.

CONTENTS

Charlie

So, my son turned eighteen yesterday. His name is Charlie. He is a gentle giant of a boy. I know that he is, on paper, a young man. It is just hard for me to get there sometimes as I have been in the front row to each of his ages. I have loved being in the front row—don't get me wrong. I am so relieved he is eighteen. And, it feels sad at the same time.

You see, he is my youngest. I now have two "adult" children. If you have been lucky enough to be where I am, you know what I am talking about. On paper, he is an "adult." In life, he is the same kid as he was the day before. Our culture, our "system," sees him differently as of yesterday. He has protections and rights and consequences now. All of them are greater. I can tell he senses it, too.

Three weeks ago, we had a brief conversation (as they all have been brief since he turned thirteen) about his upcoming birthday. I said, "You know that after that day, I can't save you" (not that I could before, but I believed I could. We all believe many things that aren't true…more on that later). "You are in a whole different league." He and I both knew what we were saying. That there are greater consequences for an eighteen-year old than a seventeen-year-old in our society's eyes. His response? "Mom, so basically what you're saying to me is that I have three weeks to do whatever I want? Get it all over with before I turn eighteen?" Yep. That is EXACTLY what I am saying. Game on.

I am not sure if he really did anything. And, I may never know. That is something else I have learned. It is okay for me not to know.

1

Knowing is a burden. It is his job to experiment and explore as it is one of the human needs we have. The problem in parenting is that it is all good to experiment and explore, when we're talking toddlers playing in sprinklers or picking up cigarette butts on the ground to honor their innate curiosity. Disgusting and understandable. And INNOCENT and maybe harmless. It is a WHOLE different ballgame for a teenager to experiment and explore. It can be life threatening. That is why we parents hold our breath during these teenage years. Praying that their experimentation and exploration does not have permanent or lifelong consequences. The stakes are high. We know it. They don't.

So, somehow we all got him to age eighteen. Why am I sad? Why did I have tears on and off all day? Because it is over. Childhood. His. And mine, being a mom to "children." I clearly am grieving. For YEARS, when asked if I had kids, I would answer, "Yes, I have two small children." Then, when they were teenagers, I realized I couldn't say that anymore. So, I stopped. What did I say then? Well, basically that I am a "parenting expert" on my knees with teenagers. Humbled. Stumbling. Finding my way through. Trying to save myself and my marriage. I was only successful on one of those fronts.

The teenage years of parenting are their own beast. I had a wise mother of a teen YEARS ago in my parenting class try to tell me this. She BEGGED for me to offer a special class just for parents of teens. I didn't have teenagers then, so how could I teach a class about teens? I had no idea what she was talking about. Yet, I could feel her desperation. I could feel the realness of it all. I knew it was ahead of me. As of yesterday, it is now behind me. Whew.

I did the best I could. I know that. I also know where I failed. There is SO much I would do differently now if I could teleport myself with all my experience back to start over with these two beautiful souls. I would be more present. I would be kinder. I would be less task-oriented and more playful. More BE, less DO. I hope that I would anyway.

I can't wait to be a grandparent. Do-over. Even better, though—a do-over without all the responsibility! Just indulge and love and play with and I won't have to groom ANYTHING in them. It will not be my job. It will be the parents' job. I can't wait. But now, let's go on a little journey back to a time when I, too, was faced with the challenge of raising little people, and show you a way through that I hope will give you permission to be human. A human parenting in the best way you possibly can.

Not perfect.

The Philosophy

*Our prime purpose in this life is to help others. And,
if you can't help them, at least don't hurt them.*
– Tenzin Gyatso, the 14th Dalai Lama (b. 1935)

The Dalai Lama speaks regularly at fundraising events, and naturally, there is great anticipation to his speeches among the waiting crowds. At one such event, His Holiness shuffled up to the podium and said, "Love each other." And then proceeded to sit back down.

The crowd was surprised as they had expectations that his speech would be a bit longer. A moment later he shuffled back up to the podium and said, "And if you can't do that, then at least don't hurt each other."

Love pretty much boils down to that. It's a practical philosophy that's been the bedrock of my life, parenting, and coaching for as long as I can remember.

Sometimes celebrities get it right: "I never said it would be easy; I only said it would be worth it," Mae West taught me.

I've had that quote posted on my bathroom mirror through many years of parenting Charlie and Grace. It's been a constant reminder that the job we are tasked with when we take home this infant is daunting. We're expected to groom in our children traits that they don't necessarily start out with. We're expected to groom cooperation, accountability, honesty, responsibility, grit, integrity, a work ethic and on and on and on.

Every person who has ever raised a child knows it is hard. Not hard like learning algebra hard; HARD like tying your shoe while bicycling in traffic going uphill blindfolded kind of hard. And, of course, life is hard.

Being alive on this planet is hard.

Going out to eat in public without worrying you could be at the mercy of a deranged gunman is hard. Pandemics are hard. Eliminate parenting from it, and simply existing is hard. But, when you add the unrelenting responsibility of raising kids to the mix, it can feel like you're part of an out of control circus where you miraculously play all the parts: ringmaster, zookeeper, high wire walker, concession stand operator, and funny man to keep everyone entertained.

Parenting definitely feels like a circus at times. Maybe even most of the time. A circus where you are responsible for the most precious angels you will ever encounter in your whole life.

Talk about pressure.

Remember the moment of panic you experienced after you had your first child? We all can recall a certain terrifying moment in time. Maybe it was at the hospital, or in the car, or the minute you arrived home with your newborn. It was the moment you thought or even verbalized, "What are you thinking giving me this kid? I don't know what I'm doing and have no business being in charge here!"

We've all had it.

Welcome to the club.

Here is the good news: You get eighteen whole years to get it right. So, really, if today was not great, you can focus on tomorrow. Parenting is hard because it is long. It is never-ending and every single day brings its own set of challenges. Some days you get it right and you get a gold star. Other days, you get the dunce cap and feel like the biggest loser on the planet. This experience molds you and changes you one back-breaking moment at a time. Like landscape etched by erosion, water, and time, you end your eighteen years as a parent completely transformed from the person you were when you started. How that looks, no one can predict. Reaching the finish line with your self-esteem intact is possible, but certainly not a guarantee.

That is the goal: To launch your kids equipped with the greatest skills to lead healthy, fruitful lives. Lives where one day they, too, may choose to walk the gauntlet of parenthood and you get to quietly wish them luck because, damn, it is hard. Really, no one can prepare you for that. If any of us were told the truth about parenting, the planet would cease to be populated. Parents would be called "masochists" or "martyrs" and really we would ALL be the worse for it.

Why? Because the experience of parenting is also like being a slab of marble carved into a masterpiece by an artist's hand. The joy of your children's laughter, the pride of knowing you helped bring forth good human beings cannot be underestimated.

And, of course, there is the knowing that you did it.

That you climbed the proverbial mountain and came down the other side a better version of yourself than when you started.

Parenting is the hardest job you'll ever love. Didn't the Marines start that? The truth is, most of us parents want to be good parents. You get the two blue stripes on the pregnancy test and experience the joy of the possibility of having this little one in your life. It starts with joy. And then the reality sets in. This is hard. It is a new kind of tired. And, you thought you knew tired before pregnancy and kids. It's a physical tired that hits during those first two years. So much caretaking. Literally, our job is to keep them alive. Keep them from unknowingly killing themselves with all kinds of dangers they are completely oblivious to. You race after them. Shepherd them. Coddle, love, snuggle, play, and witness the delight and joy each new discovery brings them.

And then they start to talk.

That's when it all changes.

True parenting, to me, doesn't really start until then. When the child begins to talk, we must raise our game. It's no longer simply caretaking. We feed and care for our dogs. We feed and care for our babies.

Neither talk much.

And then one of them finds a voice.

Game on.

Parenting has now begun.

What am I supposed to do when they tell me NO all the time?

What do I do when they won't get in the car?

Or buckle their seatbelt?

What do I do when they won't eat?

Or sit down?

Or come inside?

Or leave the pool?

What about when they hit their grandma?

Or hit me?

Or lie?

Or get out of their bed?

Or run loose at Target?

And on and on and on.

And those are only the first few years of "parenting" unknowns. More uncertainty follows in the coming years. And the years after that. And the years after that.

And then? We get to navigate the teenage years! Woohoo! I think you can see where I'm going with this—if we don't get things under control now, we're in for years of trouble and pain.

I mistakenly believed that after they turned eighteen, much of my job was done. I have since learned I was wrong. We are never done being the parent. The ages change. The stages change. The relationship changes. And, we will always be the parent. Even though they don't want us to be much of the time.

We love our kids and desperately want to get this parenting gig right. We go to sleep with guilt, wishing today went differently, committed to doing better tomorrow.

Tomorrow I will definitely not react.

I will not say those hurtful words.

I will be more patient.

I will not yell.

It's going to be different tomorrow.

Why is this parenting thing so hard?

If you're a parent under enormous amounts of stress, this book can free you to do the least amount of damage to your child. This book is for parents who want to stop losing their minds trying to raise perfect kids. Parents who are a few steps away from throwing in the towel and saying, "Sure you can eat dessert for dinner, I no longer care." Or, "I'm going to have one more drink, one more cigarette, one more Ambien because I just cannot deal with this shitshow anymore."

On the losing end of the exhaustion that comes with parenting is a surrender that all too many parents experience where they slowly give up and give in to the demands of their kids. "I want another cell phone, car, headset, video game, candy, YouTube video, book, not to do my homework" …more, more, more, and on and on and on.

When pushed too far, we parents make bad decisions.

When tired, we make bad decisions.

When stressed, we make bad decisions.

Parents either push back (too firm) or give in (too kind). Both are unhelpful and create the opportunity for their kids to go the inch and demand the next mile.

Bad parenting happens when parents feel lost for other choices. When your resources and reserves are tapped, how can you be a good parent? Especially when all you want to do is crawl back into bed and yell at the heavens, "WWWHHHHHYYYYYY?"

The simple answer is that you can't.

I used to think that as a psychotherapist AND parenting coach for over twenty years, I would be able to prevent my children from needing therapy in their futures if I did a really REALLY good job. (I really thought that.)

I gave that up ten years into the job.

I began to save for therapy instead.

Truth is, this had nothing to do with them and EVERYTHING to do with me! No matter how noble my intentions, how patient or resourced I was, I still messed up.

Often.

We are all faulty parents.

Imperfect.

No one is great all the time.

Not even me.

You know the "intention/perception" concept we counselors like to teach? It is that no matter what our intention is, the perception of our message is out of our hands. Every person we speak to—child, spouse or friend—has their own filter of life experiences through which they hear our message.

We fail.

I failed.

And, it is all still okay.

Often, being a good parent is about making the least worst decision (from our often "low resourced" state) than it is about making the best decision.

Tomorrow IS going to be different.

This book will show you how.

The simple concept I'm going to show you will bring more peace to your home and to you, quicker than you ever thought possible.

This book is a shortcut.

You do have choices. We lose when we make it so complicated.

Life is complicated.

This is not.

Here's how to use it.

The model in this book is about "Staying Away from Option D." Taking each moment one at a time and simply doing the least worst thing based on your resources and your abilities. Some days you can do more and you want to do more. Others, you are hungry, moody, and really need a break when your anxious teen needs to talk. In those moments, staying away from D is all you can do. A C-level performance is better than truly screwing up.

This is where this book comes in.

In my experience, parents need permission.

They need permission to be themselves and perfectly human and perfectly flawed and perfectly messy and perfectly the right person to be the parent for their specific kid(s), at a time when they have limited time and limited energy.

The trouble is, most parents don't feel adequate or equipped to be the parent their kid needs. Many have shared with me that the moment they lay their head on the pillow at night, the rambling thoughts of guilt and regret begin. I had them too.

The minute you have a child, you begin to have parent guilt.

Did I do enough?

Did I spend enough time with my kids today?

Did I give them what they needed?

Was I a helicopter parent?

Do they know they are loved?

Did I spend too much time at work today?

Am I being a good role model?

What can I do to ease their burdens?

Do they have friends?

Are kids being nice to them?

Are they learning enough?

What else can I do?

And on and on and on.

Today's parents have no shortage of negative self-talk opportunities when it comes to their role as a mom or dad, nor do they ever run out of "improvements" they could make if they only had enough time, resources, or energy to be a "better" parent.

Guilt settles in the moment you have a child.

The trouble with this kind of thinking is twofold: One, it's never ending. There is no solution to the litany of tasks or to-dos on a parent's plate. Each day brings new things they must accomplish or there is some looming consequence they must endure if they don't "get it together" and do a better job.

The second issue is there is never a break, so the parent who feels chronically bad or bad at parenting never gets the relief of a day off or a time-out. Instead, it's like an endless wave that keeps crashing on them day in and day out, reminding them that they're imperfect and their failures will have a forever impact on the kids they love.

It's enough to make a sane person say, "I'm NEVER going to be a parent!"

Except, parenting is full of rewards—gifts and treasures you could never experience except through the gauntlet of parenting. The thing is, you have to survive the journey if you are to reap the rewards.

So, what's a parent to do?

First, you have to accept that you're never going to get it right 100 percent of the time. You may not even get it right fifty percent of the time. But, if you adopt a model of "do no harm," things will get better.

Parents need permission.

Permission to be themselves. To be flawed, to mess up, to make mistakes. And, these mistakes are ALL GOOD for our kids. We can model mistakes and the ability/freedom to make them and show our kids how to handle them. Wisdom is gained from mistakes. Learning comes from those hard knocks. We remember and feel and live in the consequences of our own decisions.

We can come back from those. The majority of bad decisions we make in life are not permanent. They can be repaired. In doing so, we get back into integrity with ourselves.

This book is to gift parents with "grace"... and this grace is for ourselves. We are absolutely doing the best we can given the context of the moment. And when we go beyond that grace and REALLY mess up, this simple concept helps bring us back to our innate goodness. To our love for our children and our love for ourselves. It shows us how to fail and come back from it.

Perfectly imperfect permission

Most of us were not given that as kids: perfectly imperfect permission. The experience of KNOWING you are loved and cherished EVEN WHEN YOU MESS UP. Those of you out there who had this, what a special gift you had. Another term for it is "unconditional love." And, this book is applying unconditional love to ourselves. No need to beat yourself up into some kind of shame spiral.

We can interrupt that.

As I have worked with parents over the last twenty years, I have seen how this permission for imperfection frees them. It shows in their body language when they come back to see me after applying the model of "Stay away from Option D." They have a skip in their step. They are smiling. They feel good about themselves.

They are proud.

My hope is that you can have this kind of pep in your step too.

> Perfectly imperfect permission:
> The experience of KNOWING you are loved and cherished
> EVEN WHEN YOU MESS UP.

Why the solutions need to be simple

Parenting is complicated. We live in a complex world that can change on a dime from the hours of 6 a.m. to 7 a.m. There's just too much going on. When you layer into our already massively complex lives the desire to parent our kids—parent them WELL, not lose ourselves—mistakes happen.

Endless. Mistakes. Happen.

So, the answers need to be easy. Easy to access, easy to find the words for, easy to remember, easy to get back to, and easy to forgive. That's the model.

As easy as A-B-C-D.

If you've ever attended a twelve-step meeting, the floor is often littered with slogans. "Keep it simple" is one that everyone knows and can apply to almost any aspect of their sobriety. The same is true for this model.

I offer you a model that is just like your grading scale at school, minus the "F" of course.

The concept is simple. When it comes to the interactions we have daily with our children, we have options A through D. They range from the best, healthiest options to the really bad option we tend to regret on our pillows at night.

As parents, we exist among this range of four options, A through D. Our goal is to exist primarily in the A's to C's and stay away from the D's. We need to learn what causes us to descend into the D's so we can learn better ways without all the pain of years of therapy or groups or books or treatment centers. Believe it or not, you can do this all on your own with this simple little book as your guide.

The concept is so simple it's revolutionary: We have options on how we react in each of the parenting situations we find ourselves in with our kids. You didn't know you had options, did you?

Well, you do. You have four options, A through D.

These are the four types of options available to every human being in every situation we face with our kids. All parenting responses fall into one of these four categories. Think of this concept as a handy toolkit containing just four simple tools.

Here is the philosophy:

A:

Option A is the creative, long-term, textbook, well-resourced, proactive, **BEST**-case scenario, perfect-parenting option when we have the time/energy/resources to do it—which we don't always have. It's the deluxe response, you could say. It is encouraging to know that A exists. And, we need to have A uploaded into our brains so that when we have the opportunity and resources to use it, it's an accessible tool in our toolbox. We have to *learn* the A's since the only "parenting" class we got was the class to get them OUT!

Consider that A is one of four options.

It's not expected at every opportunity or interaction with our kids and it's not realistic to be doing A every time. Yet, many parents have that expectation of themselves—to be delivering A at all times. And, anything less than A means they're failing or don't measure up to what every OTHER parent out there is projecting all over their Instagram or Facebook accounts.

Perfect parenting is a myth. We cannot possibly do A at every turn as we are human, and as such, are flawed and we mess up. Humans get tired, worn out, worn down. Human parents have jobs, and bosses, and more than one child sometimes, and homes to clean, and kids to drive, and lawns to mow, and dentist appointments to get everyone to.

Option A exists. And *sometimes we can do it.*

The expectation here, though, is that an A response is not necessary *every* time. AND, we need to learn what the A's are if we are EVER going to have any hope of exercising them. We need to have them uploaded into our heads. Instead, what most of us have uploaded into our heads is that which was done to us. And, our partners have uploaded into *their heads that which was done to them.*

We parents do what we do because we are out of ideas. Not because we are malicious or want to do harm to our children.

We are simply OUT OF IDEAS.

So, we spank.

We yell.

We shame.

We guilt.

We punish.

This is not because we want to behave this way and do harm to our children.

We are simply out of ideas.

Option A provides those ideas. It's the absolute best of them all. A is the choice where you can stretch and learn and then *sometimes* implement when you have the time, patience, thought, and sleep.

Do A.

Homerun.

Effective.

Often peaceful.

Each future chapter in this book is dedicated to those Option A responses. We honor A responses with great awe and humility. Learning and knowing these A responses is part of our professional development for this job of parenting that we ALL are so unprepared for!

B:

Option B is **GOOD** parenting.

Not fully resourced, but still a great option.

It is the "good enough" response.

If we think of a scale of 1 through 10 with 10 being the A option, then B is like the 6, 7, or 8 on that scale.

It is good enough.

We are okay here, as parents.

It may be all we've got in the moment, given the context of ALL that's going on for us at the time.

It's the "give yourself a break" option. When you pull out a B response, it's "good enough," given that there was little sleep, another child crying, a traveling spouse, and it was time to leave the house.

B parenting is the "best I could do" option when I was sick.

B is the "best I could do when I was hangry."

B is still taking care of our kids. Well.

B parenting has been around for generations.

It is the "ease up on yourself" option.

You've done alright.

No guilt.

C:

Option C is **DO NO HARM.**

Walk away.

Say nothing.

Support yourself.

Augment. Fill your bucket of resources with some self-care.

Get out of the room.

Take a walk.

Breath. (Three times, DEEPLY.)

Calm yourself.

Let it go.

Listen to music.

Get something to eat.

Go outside.

Take care of yourself.

Move away.

It can *even* mean locking yourself in the bathroom or bedroom so you do not do D. Consider it your OWN time out! It's the last resort before disintegrating into D. It is literally the "give yourself a break" option.

You are still in the "perfect" parenting range here with C. C parenting is when you recognize that you're having an experience or emotion that is going to impact another person. There is an awareness that if I do not do something different here, I might be doing D shortly. I am REALLY low on resources and that is nobody's to manage but my own. I need to know myself here. And I need to help myself here. More grace given. Because, in helping ourselves (by leaving the room or doing whatever we need to do to calm ourselves, we ARE helping our child).

We have stayed away from Option D.

D:

Option D is **HARM**.

D is the only unacceptable option.

D is yelling, humiliating, hurting, shaming, spanking.

D moves are not measured responses but rather the uncontrolled reactions we have. They're the words or actions we often regret as we go to sleep at night—or thirty seconds after they come out of our mouths. Or the instant it comes out of our mouths.

D is losing it.

If we can raise our awareness to prevent D, then we can move up to C. In doing so, we can feel very good about ourselves and our parenting. D parenting may be the type of parenting you were modeled. And it may be unconscious. Many times, I have been told by adults (sharing with pride), "I was spanked and look how I turned out!"

True. You turned out just fine.

The real curiosity I have in those moments is how you felt about the yelling, the shaming, the spanking that occurred? And how do you feel about delivering it now to your own children? There are options beyond D.

This simple concept provides THREE!

D is not the only one we have at our disposal; we now have three alternatives.

D is the only unacceptable option here.

A through C responses ALL work. And, they feel really good to deliver.

Remind yourself: A, B and C ALL WORK!

The goal is **not** an A every time.

THE GOAL IS AVOIDING D.

So, our new definition of success lies in the range of these options.

It doesn't have to *be* perfect.

It doesn't have to *look* perfect.

It doesn't have to *feel* perfect.

The intent of this book is to give you permission to exist among A through C and to forgive yourself when D happens. It is also permission to celebrate that we don't have to be doing A all the time.

Perfect parenting is not the goal.

A, B, and C are all viable options. Stay away from Option D and the job you're doing is the best it can possibly be.

A through C. Any of the three are equally successful. And, maybe you need to internalize this definition of success: Being proud of yourself for your response, given the context of ALL that was occurring. It may not have worked out perfectly on the child side, but WE are clean with our words and actions.

No guilt.

We have permission to exist among A through C.

They all work.

Stay away from D and you're a "perfEct" parent.

Stay away from Option D and you will be okay.

Stay away from Option D and THEY will be okay.

That is where the pep comes from.

And the relief.

A word on spanking. No one really likes to spank. For the last twenty years, I've been teaching a five-week parenting class. When asked if they like to spank, no parent has ever raised their hand to say, "I like to spank!"

Rather, spanking typically occurs because parents are out of ideas.

They don't know what else to do, so they spank. They reacted out of frustration.

Spanking is Option D.

When other options are learned, there is no more need to spank. Consider it as one of the tools in your toolbox if you're using it. By the end of this book, you might feel resourced enough to let it go permanently and substitute other tools.

Make no mistake, it is harm.

And, it is hypocritical.

We lose credibility when we spank. We expect our children to not hit their siblings, friends, dogs, and cousins.

Yet, we spank them?

It doesn't compute in a child's mind. They're looking at what we do, not what we say.

Stay away from Option D and you'll be okay.

And now a word on when D does occur. You CAN come back from it and still be okay. Repair it. Show remorse. Make amends. Hug. Apologize to that beautiful, small human being in front of you. Humble yourself. You messed up. Admit it. Take some action to apologize or remedy the situation. Say the words AND take the action.

> ## SPANKING IS OPTION D.
> ### Stay away from Option D and you'll be okay.

There is beauty in this. The beauty is in what is modeled. The message modeled for the child is that even when you are "big" and "grown up," it is normal to make mistakes. And, the parent is showing the child how to repair mistakes. Most of them can be repaired. Most of the mistakes we make in our day to day lives are temporary and not permanent mistakes.

One of my favorite quotes on parenting is from Ralph Waldo Emerson.

"Who you are speaks so loudly that I can't hear anything that you are saying."

So, when you repair your mistake or regret, your child is watching this. They are learning from this. They see that it's okay to make mistakes. They see it's not only children who are learning. Adults are learning too. This message is profound.

> "Who you are speaks so loudly that I can't hear anything that you are saying."
> - Ralph Waldo Emerson

Now you have it. A through D. Throughout the rest of this book, we will look at real-world examples from each of those options.

You'll learn A techniques—the best-case scenario,

B techniques—pretty darn good,

C examples—do no harm, and

D reactions—avoid at all costs!

Armed with these tools in your toolkit, you can carry this simple concept with you into as many parenting AND life situations as you want. Take it. Remind yourself. Forgive yourself. Let go. Know you have power in what you choose to do. When you're able to pause and think, it's no longer a REACTION—it's a RESPONSE. Reactions have no thought. They are the words and actions we say or do impulsively and often immediately that we regret. IF we can PAUSE, then the A's will be more available and obvious to us to use.

And, this is how you can use this book.

Look up the A's for the situations where you would like to relieve some stress or tension in your home. Practice those.

Practice it for a while and feel relief in that situation.

Real relief.

Feel it before you move on to the next area of parenting you wish to address and change. Pace yourself. Don't overwhelm yourself. Be reasonable. In focusing your energies on one or maybe two changes, you are setting yourself up for success.

Best practices (A) are described regarding numerous parenting challenges we all face. Read the whole book or pick chapters that might apply to your current situation. Use it as a resource. Reference other chapters later when they apply to the stage you're in with your kids.

And, from what perspective am I coming? There are many styles of parenting.

Everything that follows in this book will be teaching you how to be BOTH firm and kind *at the same time*. Often, in a couple, the balancing act might be that if one tends toward firm parenting, the other feels pressure to then be the kind parent.

Good cop/bad cop.

We all know how to be FIRM. We all know how to be KIND. What we typically don't know how to do is be BOTH at the same time. And, that is exactly what our children need from us.

Firmness and kindness.

Firm and kind involve allowing the child space, for them and for us. Letting them know we are here to help or support, yet we are not going to take over and then render them feeling incapable.

It involves holding boundaries (firm) while still letting them know we care and they are loved (kind). It involves offering to help with one part of the task and allowing them the space to feel the frustration and pain of practicing something new. And, that something new may be a task we have always done for them and need to hand over to them to better prepare them in life.

Hence, why I can't wait to be a grandparent. I only need to practice kind...

And, how to prioritize these changes you wish to make?

As you implement these tools, do so *gradually*.

We parents have limited resources: time, energy, funds, information. So how do we prioritize changes we wish to implement? Our list can be loooonnnngggg. We may have various frustrations with our children ranging on one end, "This is completely dysfunctional," to "This is really inappropriate," to "There has GOT to be a better way than this," to mere irritation.

> Firm and kind involve allowing the child space, for them and for us. Letting them know we are here to help or support, yet we are not going to take over and then render them feeling incapable.

One way to think of implementing these strategies is to consider three bands. The top band contains those two or three interactions/times of day that are causing the MOST stress or strife. Dedicate your resources (time and energy) to changing those moments for yourself AND for your family. Doing this will deliver the most relief and even peace. When those have been minimized or eradicated, then we can move down to the middle band. This band contains those interactions that we KNOW are not okay, but we just don't have the energy to deal with them currently. With more time and practice, we can move down to the bottom band of irritants. These are tweaks and will continue to surface as our children developmentally change and grow. In the words of Stephen Covey, "Keep first things first"—the most stressful need to be relieved first before we move down the list.

MOST STRESSFUL
(Those 1-2 situations that are causing you the most stress or strife. Focus here first.)

THESE ARE <u>NOT</u> OKAY
(And, I don't have the energy to focus on these until relieving the most stressful band above.)

TWEAKS
(These are not urgent, causing chaos, or stress AND they need our attention when we relieve previous two bands.)

And, we might just feel peace.

For your situation, bedtime may be the highest stressor in your day, and thus a red flag that it may not be the best time to try to implement new strategies you learn in this book. If you are not ready to implement and stay committed to the strategy, then perhaps reconsider trying or beginning it when you ARE ready and committed. Save yourself and your energy. And, be able to pass the baton without criticism if you have a partner who can take over for you. No judgment. This gig brings us face to face with ourselves. It humbles us. Through it, we learn how to be unselfish. Give yourself a break. Be smart. Implement when YOU have the resources to change the dance you're doing. It will take effort and patience and likely repetition/consistency. So, do it when you have those within you to offer.

Improvement, not perfection.

Improvement, not perfection.
Improvement, not perfection.
That is our goal.

Voltaire said, "Don't let perfect be the enemy of the good." Good enough is what we are striving for here, not perfection. Option A is wonderful to know about and sometimes to implement. It is not, however, realistic to have it be our goal in every interaction. Don't let perfect be the enemy of the good.

And, what does success look like?

Success here is defined as when YOU, the parent, feel good about what you have done. THEN, you are successful. We often think success means the interaction worked out beautifully or seamlessly for both parties, parent and child. Not so. It may look like a hot mess and YOU, the more resourced of the two parties, can feel really good about your role as a mom or dad.

For instance, the bedtime routine can look quite ugly if objectively observed as the child is melting down, low resourced and simply needs to get to bed. And, the parent could be demonstrating stellar parenting techniques. You feel good about your words and actions? Success here.

> Improvement,
> not perfection.
> -
> Improvement,
> not perfection.
> -
> Improvement,
> not perfection.

Take one tool and practice it for three to four weeks until it is natural and normal for you and for the children. Then, consider working on another. If bedtime is causing you the most stress or strife, save your energies for bringing peace to the bedtime routine. We all have limited resources of time and energy. Save your energies for the most stressful situations and find relief with those before moving down the list of areas of improvement that will also provide relief. When you finally work through the three bands and get to the bottom of your list, you will simply be tweaking. So many good practices will already be there.

And what about our dogs?

Why am I asking?

We seem to invest more in training our dogs than learning how to parent our kids.

True?

Have you invested more there?

With our kids, we took the class to get them OUT. The childbirth class. Then, we're sent home with our bundle of joy and are meant to do on-the-job-training while sleep deprived, busy, stressed, emotional. Give yourself permission, real permission, to learn that which we have never been taught.

Learn to exist among the three acceptable options with your kids: the best practice, the good enough, and the do no harm options.

This simple philosophy for parenting is also a simple philosophy for life.

As the Dalai Lama stated (and what does he know?),

"Our prime purpose in this life is to help others. And, if you can't help them, at least don't hurt them."

Stay away from option D and you will be a perfEct parent.

ONE

The Morning Rush

You're back to the self-talk on the pillow at night…
So, tomorrow is going to be different.
Tomorrow is going to be different.
Tomorrow is going to be different.

It already is because you are reading this and have the intention to do something different. Morning comes and before you ever get out of bed, breathe deeply three times (through the nose only as it activates the parasympathetic nervous system) and remind yourself, "I am 100% responsible for what I say and what I do."

If I get into one of those guilt provoking moments, I will pause and do this again—breathe deeply three more times (you just did C!). In doing so, I will no longer be reacting to my child; I will be *responding*. Responses have thought. Reactions have none. So, if I can pause long enough to breathe three times, I am giving myself the pause that yields a response. If counting works better for you, do that. It occupies the brain. Gives it something to chew on with a task of counting. Even better? Count AND breathe. In that pause, you might even be able to think of one of those new strategies and eliminate the pillow guilt.

> I am 100% responsible for what I say and what I do.

1

Success already.

•••

STRAIGHT OUT OF COLLEGE, I did a program called Teach for America. I was sent into inner city Houston and in the month of October, some overstuffed kindergarten classes created the need for a new class to be created to lower the numbers and take on the overflow. Three teachers were given the opportunity to CHOOSE eight children to give to me.

Not random.

Not last in.

Not chosen by the principal.

The teachers picked the ones they didn't want. Needless to say, I was not set up to succeed. I was given these twenty-four beautiful children and sent to an outside trailer. One child was mute. I swear I could have been teaching them devil worship and no one would have known. Or cared. I worked SO HARD at not reacting. I was twenty-two years old and had no idea what I was doing. My most common intervention that kept me from Option D?

I chewed on the ends of pens.

Hard.

There were many altered pens.

I am not sure what I taught them or if they even learned anything.

I do know what they felt, though.

They felt loved.

Whatever Ms. Gambs lacked in experience and knowledge, she tried to make up for with love. And, it required a WHOLE lot of pen chewing for me. I did my best to stay away from Option D.

Remember: Success for us here is not that the situation worked out perfectly or that you did A. It is NOT that the situation is seamless or beautiful or textbook. Success is NOT that your child does exactly what you want. Rather, success is that you're proud (okay, maybe not proud), but okay and clean with your own words and behaviors with your child. No regrets. Your child may in fact be having a "perfect tantrum" and be melting down, but *you* know the way you responded with your words and actions was good and acceptable, causing no harm and leaving no feelings of regret at the end of the day.

Success.

Congratulations.

You've come a long way, baby.

So, to really let that sink in, success here is not that the situation is seamless or beautiful or textbook. Rather, success is determined by you feeling good about your words and actions, thereby yielding a guilt-free ending to your day when your head hits the pillow.

> Success is YOU feeling proud of your words and behaviors, not that the situation worked out perfectly.

So, now the child wakes up and you have already reset your nervous system to be more ready to receive them. You have breathed intentionally a few times through your nose and are now squarely in the parasympathetic nervous system (the calming relax, restore one) and not in the sympathetic (fight, flight, freeze). You have something to give. Depositing in your own tank first. Relationships are like that: emotional bank accounts, according to Stephen Covey. We deposit into them by doing good things for our souls, and make withdrawals from them when we're in stressful situations. In order to make a withdrawal, there has to be something actually in the account.

What are deposits?

For yourself?

For your child?

Deposits for you may be large or small. Perhaps it is a walk in nature first thing in the morning. A favorite hot drink for yourself to start your day. Journaling. A massage. Lunch with a friend. Exercise.

•••

DURING THE FIRST YEAR OF MY SON'S LIFE, I stayed home full time with Grace and Charlie. She was in her two-three year and he wasn't yet one. If you're reading this book, then you know EXACTLY what that means. There is SO very much physically to do in a day. So much caretaking. Feeding. Cleaning. Changing. Cleaning again. Feeding again. I remember breakfast would barely be cleaned up before lunch was needed. Grace was just beginning to need my inadequate parenting skills at that age of two to three. Charlie? I just needed to love him and keep him alive. In fact, Sean would check in with me throughout the day, sometimes asking if we were all still alive? That was our definition of success then.

Everybody alive?

Good.

It was exhausting.

My Granny gave great advice to me as I was staying home that year full-time with our sweet two-year-old and newborn. She said, "When the going gets rough, get something to eat or go outside."

That, my friends, is sage advice.

Simple wisdom from those ahead of us. She knew. Change your scenery. It helps. Get out in nature. It helps. Get a drink. It helps. Get a snack. It helps.

And, I found it helpful when possible to do both: Get something to eat AND go outside.

I still use that advice. In fact, I use it now while writing this book. At the end of Granny's life, I went to visit her in the assisted living facility. She was in a wheelchair at the dining room table. Not speaking anymore. I sat with her and fed her what little she would eat. And then? We rolled right out the front door into the crisp day. I sat next to her outside and teared up, knowing.

She taught me this.

"When the going gets rough, get something to eat, or go outside."

Granny will be proud of you.

Those both work for me.

Why?

Nature has a calming effect on me—the air, the colors, the beauty. It is an automatic reset. And eating. It affects my physiology. Sometimes it's just getting a drink of water that helps me shift and brings me back to myself. A deposit for my own bank account. We are trying not to be overdrawn and have to suffer the consequences that come with that. Scary mommy. Mean mommy. Regrettable words and actions.

So "your greatest good" has woken up. Today is a school day. The clock is ticking. The bus is coming.

First, do your children have an alarm clock waking them up? It helps to remove yourself from being the authority figure in as many situations as possible as we have that role enough. So rather than you, an alarm clock is an option. If not, think calm/loving "wakeup"—rub the toes, rub the back, gently open the curtains.

We want their entry to the day to be pleasant and inviting.

They are now awake.

Are they expected to dress before breakfast? If you reside in a two-story house, that may help rather than trying to send them back up for that task. Being "ready" for breakfast may mean clothes, socks and shoes or they are not "ready" for breakfast to be consumed.

•••

ONE MORNING CHARLIE CAME DOWNSTAIRS for school announcing he was "ready" for breakfast. ("Ready" at our house meant shoes, socks, clothing). He was not wearing any shoes. A natural tendency of mine before learning these tools would have been to give him a command, "You are not ready; put on your shoes." Thankfully, what came out of my mouth (that morning anyway) was "What else do you need to be ready?" He looked down at his own sweet self and announced, "Shoes!"

Yep. You go, bud. You got this.

He utilized his own God-given brain. Mine was not used.

They are capable. We just have to stop telling and reminding. Ask. Their brains kick in and they think.

Questions rather than commands.
Questions rather than commands.
Questions rather than commands.

Let's consider the differences. Imagine you're told to complete a set of tasks given in the form of commands: Get dressed, wash the car, do the dishes, vacuum the carpets. How many do you think you would do? How many might you ignore or "forget"? It is human nature. We do not like being told what to do. We all have a need for power. And, children inherently do not get a lot of power. We tell them where to go, when to go, what to say, what to wear. And we wonder why they resist us?

They resist us because they need power, too.

And, there are tasks that must get done.

What to do?
Consider questions.

There is a hierarchy here. And the hierarchy is this, from least to most effective:

- Commands.
- Closed-ended questions.
- Open-ended questions.

Open-ended questions get better results than closed-ended. Closed-ended have "yes" or "no" as their only possible responses. Examples include: "Have you brushed your teeth? Do you have your homework done? Are you dressed?" All the child is required to come up with here is a simple yes or no response. Not much reflection or thought required.

Closed-ended questions are a better option than commands.

Also, if we, as parents, are asking closed-ended questions where yes and no are the only answers, then "no" had better be an acceptable response or we are asking the wrong question. So, "Do you want to have hot dogs for dinner?" is a closed-ended question. Not having hot dogs for dinner had better work for you or you have just set yourself up for a conflict.

We do this all the time.

Including me.

We are hoping for cooperation or compliance with our closed-ended questions. And, then we are irritated or angry when we get the response, "No, I don't want hot dogs for dinner." Yet, we did it to ourselves! If hot dogs ARE for dinner, then a statement indicating that would be appropriate: "We are having hot dogs for dinner." Not, "Do you want to have hot dogs for dinner?" That is closed-ended. Yes or no are the only responses available for that question...so "no" had better work for you since you posed the question.

Another way we slide a command into a closed-ended question is when we're hoping for cooperation. We want them to like our idea. So, we add the "okay" onto the end of the sentence.

"We are having spaghetti tonight for dinner, okay?"

That began with a statement about the dinner provided being spaghetti. Then, the "okay" tacked on the end made it a closed-ended question whereby now the child can weigh in on that as acceptable or not acceptable to them!

Perhaps just drop the "okay," okay?

"We are having spaghetti for dinner tonight." (No "okay?" tacked on. No opportunity for them to say, "Not okay.")

Open-ended questions, on the other hand, require thought by the person answering the question. Often, when an open-ended question is asked, the eyes roll up in the head and the child looks up. The child is *thinking*. Actual *thinking* is required to come up with a response. For example, "What do you need to be ready?" The eyes roll up in the head as the child uses their God-given brains to come up with an answer.

They have to think.

With commands, they are spoon-fed over and over what they need to do and they do not have to use their brains. Someone *else* is using a brain and offering their own "great" ideas. More effective is for the *child* to exercise thought and consider what it is *they* need to do, like Charlie and the shoes.

I feel your pain here.

To do this requires restraint.

An easy pitfall: telling, reminding, nagging about what is omitted and still needs to be done. So, even though you can plainly see that the child has clothes on but no shoes, resist the impulse to say, "Get your shoes on."

We have got to shut up.

And not point out the obvious.

We have to zip it (the mouths) and use the open-ended, thought-provoking question, "What do you need to be ready?"

> "What do you need to be ready?"

Back to the dinner question. Open-ended sounds like, "What would you like to have for dinner?" Perhaps that might be too open-ended for you. A middle option would be to offer a choice: "Would you like pizza or hot dogs for dinner?"

Choices give the child power.

And, they desperately need some of that.

A note on power.

Remember: Children inherently do not get a lot of power. We tell them where to go, when to go, what to wear, with whom they are going and we wonder why they resist us?

Children are littler, they are not lesser.

That bears repeating: Children may be littler, but they are not lesser.

They are small versions of us. Future adults.

The belief that they are lesser human beings is outdated and is now retired. It *used* to be that children were "meant to be seen and not heard." We know so much more about child development and the brain now to know that children have the same needs as children in adult bodies have. They are simply smaller versions of us. And our needs, in big bodies or small bodies, are: the need for belonging, the need for power, the need to feel special/valued/important, the need to give and receive love, and the need to experiment and explore. Power is one of these needs. We parents have so very much power over children by our sheer size. We are intimidating.

Have you ever stood next to an NBA player? They are giants compared to the average American. This is how our children see us—as giant NBA players. Think about it. It can be rather intimidating. How important and valued a small person feels when that giant bends down or squats down to listen eye to eye to them.

That is powerful.

Humbling.

> ## Children are littler, they are not lesser.

When did your parents come down to your eye level? Usually it was with squinted, angry eyes when you were in some kind of trouble. It was not out of respect for you as a small person, wanting you to feel at ease and not intimidated or overpowered. Eye level levels the playing field. It is respectful. So, come down to listen to your child. Come down to speak to your child. It shows humility and respect for these beautiful beings.

And, you might even have less yelling at your house by making this *one* tweak. It has happened in my world.

Many, many times.

Children are littler; they are not lesser.

Back to the morning routine. "Are you ready for breakfast?" Now this question implies that the child knows what "ready" means.

It may be time well spent to invest in some brainstorming what "ready" means. At your house, it might be three, four, or five tasks. Smaller children can create a picture key of those items so they can go reference a visual guide of what they still need to do (another way of taking you out of being the authority figure). Pictures of them actually *doing* the tasks or simply using cut-out magazine pictures of a pair of shoes, a pair of socks, clothing, toothbrush, breakfast, backpack or whatever defines "ready" in your home.

The same concept may be applied to the evening routine before bed. The child has a visual key they can go reference to see if they are "ready" for bed. This will eliminate you being the broken record that provides the answers of what else they need to do. It eliminates them appearing absent-minded, when, in fact, they are not.

When you hear yourself being the broken record relaying the same words over and over again, are you sick of hearing yourself? It's a safe assumption your child is sick of hearing it, too. That was my clue to myself that I needed to do something different in that situation as it was clearly not working!

"For every child who forgets, there is a parent who remembers." ~Barbara Colorosa.

She is on to something.

> For every child who forgets,
> there is a parent who remembers.
> - Barbara Colorosa

So, we parents must stop being the memory so our children can exercise their own minds.

Barbara Colorosa also said, "Nagging makes it your problem; silence makes it theirs."

Problems have owners. When we nag, we are owning the problem. When we are silent on it, often the ownership of the problem gets transferred back to the rightful owner. Reminding Charlie of the need to put his shoes on makes it my problem.

Being silent on the shoes makes it his problem.

Problem solved.

How to Handle the Morning Rush, Options A to D

A - Ideal: Ask open-end questions. "What do you need to be ready?" "What *else* do you need to do to be ready?"

B - Good: Ask yes or no questions. "Have you brushed your teeth?" "Are you dressed yet?" "Do you have your shoes on?" "Have you had breakfast?" or any other yes or no questions (closed-ended)

C - Do no harm: Tell them what to do, the list they ignored: Get dressed, brush your teeth, eat breakfast. This option will create a dependency on you. You become their memory and they are not exercising their own mind and are robbed of an opportunity to feel capable.

D - Harm: Yelling at them what to do (the above list in a loud, overpowering, shaming, scary voice), shaming them for not being ready, threatening them with a punishment after school.

Stay away from option D and you will be a perfEct parent.

TWO

Setting Limits

Why is it so hard for us to set limits? Why is it so hard for our kids to receive them? It's an odd dichotomy with limits.

We have trouble delivering them, yet our children are starving for them.

And, they resist them at the same time.

Despite appearances, limits make our children feel safe. They don't *really* want to be in charge. They understand on some deeper level that they are dependent and desperately need our courage, strength and wisdom. They know they need to lean on us.

Boundaries provide our children that safety. When they're small, their physical boundary might be a playpen to keep them safe. As they demonstrate their maturing abilities, their physical limit might be a room with a gate enclosing it. Eventually, when they master stairs, the physical limit might be the whole first floor. The boundaries expand based on the behaviors and maturity of the child. If they demonstrate a violation of that boundary, then it gets smaller again. Back they go in the playpen.

This advance/retreat concept is the same as they age.

Teenagers demonstrating good judgment with the car and coming home by curfew may be allowed at times to extend the curfew for special events. Those violating curfew might find themselves "back in the playpen" with an earlier curfew.

Whenever a limit is set, expect for it to be tested. If not, be pleasantly surprised.

That bears repeating.

Whenever you set a limit for your child, expect the child to test it. If they do not, be pleasantly surprised.

Your child needs to test you to see if you're credible or not... if you mean it. If they don't test you, consider yourself lucky and credible!

And, if you're no longer tested, perhaps you have established credibility with your child! Congratulations!

You *earned* that credibility.

They know you mean what you say and have less need to test the limit.

But, what do you do when they test the limit? You've set a boundary and they have crossed it.

First, what NOT to do. When they test the limit you've just communicated, no lecture is necessary.

> Whenever a limit is set, expect for it to be tested.
> If not, be pleasantly surprised.

So, let's say they pushed past the limit, and we start in with "I told you I would be shortening your curfew by thirty minutes for every fifteen you were late" in an exasperated tone. Now, they have a new target to offload their energy: the lecture you're giving and the tone in which you're giving it! That becomes their focus instead of where it needs to be, which is on their violation of the curfew you set.

They won. They have successfully deflected any accountability or wrongdoing and have now redirected the conversation to what YOU are doing wrong.

No need for words or lectures—just do it.

Deliver the consequence you promised previously with your limit or whatever the necessary one is now that the limit has been violated. Preferably with a calm voice. "Your curfew is now thirty minutes earlier."

Instead of the old adage, "If I have told you once, I have told you a thousand times!" perhaps try telling them once, and then follow through a thousand times. With gentleness and calm. If not, you're going to lose when they choose to focus on your tone and delivery instead of their violation.

> Try telling them once, and then follow through a thousand times.

That is A—delivering any parenting messages with a calm voice.

It is so hard to maintain our calm when all our emotions are triggered by these beautiful beings!

This sense of calm and the delivery of our limits with cool composure is even more paramount with teenagers. Michael Bradley wrote a book, *Yes, Your Teen is Crazy*. You want to know the one HUGE takeaway for me from that book?

The need for us parents to become what he calls a "dispassionate cop."

I love this.

And, it is so very true.

Here's why.

The cop part is easy to understand. Deliver the consequences.

•••

I AM A SPEEDER. FOR REAL. I love driving fast. I always have. I like to think I'm actually European and was born in the wrong place. If I lived in Europe, my driving would be considered normal there. My average speed I seem to continually find myself going is eighty-two miles per hour. It feels natural to me.

I can try and be conscious and slow myself down. And, no matter what, I end up back at eighty-two.

"Here is your speeding ticket, Ms. Gambs."

"Thank you, officer."

I've gotten speeding tickets many times in my life. The simple consequence of my speeding. It is not usually a happy or welcomed moment for me. I deserved the ticket on each occasion.

I am accountable for speeding.

I did it.

I violated the law.

I broke the limit.

And, I also know I have done this countless other times, (probably hundreds) and have *not* been caught and given a ticket. So, I earned this moment. I earned this consequence. It rests squarely on my shoulders.

Same with these kids of ours.

If we can deliver the news of the consequence as a "dispassionate cop," the message is going to sink in effectively.

But so often, this is not what we do.

We are *passionate* in our delivery of the consequence. Or in our delivery that our limit has been violated.

These reactions from our mouths are quite common:

"I just told you _____, so why did you do that?" (shaming/blaming)

"How could you do this to me?" (sharing hurt/guilt inducing)

"Why did you just do that?" (sarcastic)

Want to know the dumbest question we ask our kids? Truly, the dumbest one?

It's "why?"

And why is it why?

It's because we're asking them a question they can't answer. They don't know why they did or said something. They truly don't. And as a much smaller-in-stature human being, the child is now looking up at the giant, who is their parent, and cannot give the giant an answer. They truly don't know why.

> The dumbest question that we ask our kids is "WHY?"

So, we parents can and should ask them questions they can answer.

For instance, they can answer, "**What** happened here?"

How did this happen?

Who did this?

When did this happen?

Where were you when this happened?

So, let's stick to who, what, when, how, and where. And, let's leave out the "why" since they truly do not have an answer for us!

They are simply trying to get their needs met: belonging, love, power, to feel special/valued/important, and to experiment/explore. Our kids are always working on one of those.

belonging

-

love

-

power

-

to feel special/
valued/important

-

to experiment/
explore

And, so are we.

Those are the same needs children in adult bodies have.

They are our needs, too.

The difference is (especially as a therapist) that an adult can often answer that question, "why?" They can be curious about themselves and reflect and come up with something.

A child usually cannot.

They are simply acting out their needs. That's why, if young kids are to be in therapy it is likely some kind of play therapy.

This is what they do—act out their needs. It's up to us to look at them through this lens of needs and understand what need they're trying to get met, and help them get it met appropriately, so they have less need to get it met inappropriately.

Dispassionate cop. Deliver the news without all the emotion. Deliver the consequence. And ask them questions they can answer, leaving out the one they can't: WHY?

So how do we do this?

How do we set limits?

According to Kathryn Kvols, author of *Redirecting Children's Behavior*, there are three steps to setting a limit:

Step 1: Empathize. Make the person (child or partner) feel heard and understood.

Step 2: State the limit clearly (with no "but" leading this statement).

Step 3: Present options. What choices does the person have?

Typically, we only do one of these steps.

We do step two—we state the limit clearly.

If step one and three are added, you'll start to see a WHOLE lot more cooperation in your house.

•••

GRACE WAS NINE YEARS OLD WHEN we were at the dermatologist to have a wart frozen off her right index finger, which she used daily to write. She had had a mole removed before. So, she knew it was going to hurt, and she was freaking out in the exam room waiting for the doctor.

I was with her in the room.

As I often did in the years raising Charlie and Grace, I talked to myself, "Michelle, you teach this stuff. What do you need to do now?" It came to me then, that she was scared and feeling powerless and needed some power back. This led me back to these three steps.

I said: "Grace, you are scared, and you know it's going to hurt." (Step 1: Empathize, make them feel heard and understood).

"We need to have this done because this is the finger you use to write with." (Step 2: State the limit clearly with no "but" at the beginning of the sentence.)

"Do you want me to stay with you in the room or wait in the hallway?" (Step 3: Offer choice or power over *something* since she has no power over Step 2).

She immediately stopped crying and said she wanted me to stay in the room with her.

She had power over something.

Power is an important need.

It gets a bad rap being associated with the term "control."

We all need power.

In Victor Frankl's written account of his imprisonment in a concentration camp, *Man's Search for Meaning*, he reflects on power/choice being the element that could not be taken from him. He had power over his attitude. He had choice over his thoughts and perspective. Even in a concentration camp where all power appears to be stripped, this man found power.

Power is *always* a need for each of us.

For our children, however, there are three stages when power is more *intensely* needed. We typically know two of them: the "terrible twos" and teens.

Right?

The third? It's age five.

•••

AT AGE FOUR, CHARLIE STARTED A stage for about a year and a half where we called him "the contrarian." Why did we call him that during this stage?

Everything we did or said, he said or did the opposite. He did this *even* when I knew he preferred or wanted my option. He opposed us to exercise his need of power.

So normal.

It became: "Mom, you can walk next to me going into school, but you can't hold my hand."

Done.

"Mom, you can lay with me at bedtime, but you can't touch me."

Okay.

Thank goodness I taught this stuff! I knew this was about power, and this was an intense age and stage for him regarding that need so I tried to give him power as often as possible in as many ways I could.

Remember, children inherently do not get a whole lot of power.

We tell them when to go, where to go, with whom, what to wear, what to say.

You likely do the same when told what to do.

And we wonder *why* they resist us.

Power.

It's helpful to keep this in mind: Your child is not *trying* to make you or your life miserable. It's not personal to you. The child is merely going through another *normal* developmental stage.

Give them as much power as possible.

What that looked like for Charlie was letting him decide or dictate when it wasn't so important for me to do so. These times were all followed with a whole lot of "okays" from me. Remember, the need for power is ever present in each of us. However, it is *more* intense at age five (and two and teen). So, give power as much as you can.

Offer choices as often you can.

> Children inherently do not get a whole lot of power...so offer choices as often you can.

Terrible twos are not always so terrible.

A child has found his/her voice and that voice has power. It has the power to make the big people crazy. Therein lies the newfound power. Before, they did not have a voice. They would throw a fit or cry and scream but words were not part of it.

Now they have words.

And, the words have power.

Especially that big word, NO.

They find joy in opposing us. It is delightful sometimes to see what the big lady is going to do when I oppose her. This can easily turn into, "No, I won't," followed by "Yes, you will," a classic power struggle. It's like we have entered a boxing arena and are duking it out. I would find myself arguing with a four- or seven-year-old like I was four or seven! How did this happen? It's so natural and easy for us to do…power struggle.

The easiest way to give power to a child is to offer choices.

Giving choices to a two-year-old who has just found their voice will help. The three steps to setting limits provide that choice in the third step. A version might sound like this to a child who wants candy before dinner:

Step one – Make them feel heard and understood. If you cannot think of anything to say, simply repeat what the child said.

You: "You really would love to have some candy? Candy tastes really good."

Step two – Set a boundary with no "but"...only a period or "and"
You: "We eat the healthy food first before dessert, at our house."
(I qualified a lot of things with that last phrase, "at our house." Then, it doesn't matter what is happening at friends' houses or Grandma's house. "At our house...")

Step three – Offer a choice to give them power
You: "Do you want to put the candy next to your plate or here on the counter until after dinner?"

> The easiest way to give power to a child is to offer choices.

There is a natural tendency to put a "but" at the end of step one. When we do that, it can disqualify what came before it. Consider this: "I love you, *BUT* could you be on time?"

Do you *really* feel loved?

An alternative is this: "I love you, *AND* could you be on time?"

How does that feel? Better, right?

How about this example from work or home: "You did such a great job on that project, *BUT* I need this one part to be changed."

Now substitute "but" with "and" or a period, and it sounds like: "You did such a great job on that project. There is this one part I need to be changed."

How does *that* feel? It lets the positive statement stand alone without anything being taken away from it.

The "but" tends to negate what came before it, often disqualifying it. It can sound patronizing. A simple shift to a period or an "and" makes a huge difference in how it is received.

Setting limits and keeping boundaries with our kids is soooo needed.

They need to receive them.

And, we need to be providing them.

Remember, boundaries make them feel safe, especially when they encounter the natural resistance that ensues from laying them down. This may not be overtly expressed or consciously acknowledged, but they want them. They want a curfew. They want to know someone cares enough about them to stand up to them. They want to feel protected. They want someone to promote healthy eating and not candy. It's comforting to know someone has their back and is helping them, so the sugar addiction won't be in charge. They want you to tell them NO on riding their bike to their friend's when they have not demonstrated savviness with the rules of the road. They want to be rested for school the next day even though they resist bedtime every night!

Tough love is still love. And boundaries can feel like tough love. You got this.

> Tough love is still love.
> And boundaries can feel like tough love.

Pause. Breathe. Remember, you DO have options here as you are trying to provide options for them! Some folks even write the three steps on their hand to remember in the moment how to execute it until it becomes natural. And it WILL become natural. Do whatever works for you. Keep going. Give yourself at least three weeks of practice before expecting it to "feel" natural. Until then, it may feel like an alien is speaking through you. With more practice, it'll start to come naturally.

Here's an example of A, the ideal response:

Step 1: Respond with some empathetic words that acknowledge you hear what your child is really saying: "You want to stay up because it's a lot more fun playing Legos (or reading, watching a movie, etc.) than it is to go to bed. That makes perfect sense to me. I sometimes find it hard too." (Step one, check.)

Step 2: State the limit clearly with no "but" at the beginning of the sentence. You may place a period or an "and" at the end. "It's eight o'clock and time for bed."

Step 3: This is where the power lies for the child. Pick ONE set of options for the child (not a litany of choices). What options are there? Examples: "Would you like to read one more page or two more pages? Would you like to wear these jammies or these jammies? Would you like (other parent) to read to you or me? Do you want oatmeal or scrambled eggs for breakfast?" It's all about choices! Note that the choice can be about the current situation OR it can be about a future option, like breakfast.

Now, it might seem like these are bribes but they aren't. They're neutral options for the child. The tone of voice is important here as well. You need to deliver your message with a poker face. FOR REAL. There should be NO indication of which preference you're leaning toward. If we can say it in a neutral tone, without bias, then it truly is a choice for them. Empowered, check. If we present the options with an obvious bias, where our voice emphasizes one of the options over the other, like, "Do you want to wear this dress or THIS dress?—then the child will naturally choose the one that wasn't your preference. Why? Power. Even though they may very well prefer the same one as you. This happens *all the time*. I trust you have seen many examples of this already in your parenting arsenal of experience.

Once you've presented the options in a non-biased manner and your child has made their choice, then, execute. Whatever option they chose.

And what happens if they DON'T choose? What do you say?

"You choose or I will choose for you."

You can even give them a courteous timeframe you're willing to wait before taking back the power and making the decision for them. E.g., "You have ten seconds to make a choice" (for smaller children, you can even quietly count backwards from ten).

For older kids or those who've already been through this process with you, you can respectfully offer a time limit. "You choose or I will choose for you. I'll give you one minute to decide" (or one day or before dinner or whatever works for you).

And then? If they STILL don't make a choice? You choose. But expect them to throw a "perfect fit." The kind where they collapse, melt down on the floor, agonize, beg. You've seen these happen at Target. It is "the perfect fit" (coined by Charlie and Grace's dad).

When this happens, DO NOT CHANGE YOUR CHOICE THAT YOU MADE FOR THEM.

> And what happens if they DON'T choose? What do you say?
> "You choose or I will choose for you."

Why? Because of the precedent you're setting for the future. This is modeling. You want to set the standard for this situation going forward. There's a protocol you are beautifully demonstrating. And what is that? It's the message that they have an opportunity to impact their own life by making a choice, and next time they might want to take that opportunity. The "perfect fit" is frustrating for them as they just had the power offered to them taken away.

And that is a hard place—to feel powerless.

This is a natural consequence of their own choice in the matter. They intuitively will understand that it rests squarely on their shoulders to do it differently NEXT time. Make the decision. Take the power. Influence their own life. They feel accountable.

The likely result of this, with repetition, is that you've established credibility and they know you mean what you say (e.g., ten seconds, one minute, before dinner) and the NEXT time this happens, they'll likely make the choice for themselves.

Beautiful execution on your part.

Dealing with a child's perfect fit is a "perfect" example of what happens when the power is removed from them. In these situations, your goal/intention is future-oriented peace. It's a long-term strategy, not so much in the moment. There will be pain in the moment.

Endure it. Know you're doing an AMAZING job. You are a stellar parent in that moment. Even though an outside observer might judge differently. You know what needs to be done to ensure that, maybe next time, your child may have learned to make a choice and avoid losing power.

Remember: What other people think of us is none of our business.

So, when you're in Target and you've established expectations before you go into the store about what you need from them once you're inside—expectations to "stay" (i.e., stay next to the cart or in the cart, stay in the same aisle as me where I can see you, it's my job to keep you safe and I get scared when I can't see you)—and your child defies those boundaries, what do you do? Leaving your cart and leaving Target with an hysterical child IS beautiful parenting. Despite what is observed by onlookers.

Why? Because now you're credible to your child. The next time you go to Target and revisit these expectations in the car before you go in, they have this experience to draw upon and know you mean it.

•••

CHARLIE WAS THREE AND WOULD NOT get ready for "kids' day," as we called day care. For us, some days were "mommy days" and some days were "kids' days." On this day, I gave him opportunities to get dressed before we left the house. He did not accept these opportunities. So, I let him know we would be leaving regardless of whether he had gotten dressed or not.

He had not.

So, we left.

He was in his (darling) pajamas.

He panicked a bit in the car.

We arrived at kids' day and the panic blossomed. More like hysteria. The long walk down the corridor to his room was filled with his anguished cries. And, as a parenting coach, I had been hired by this daycare to deliver workshops for their staff.

For many years.

I was not anonymous.

And, now I have this screaming child (darling as he was in his jammies) announcing our visibly incomplete arrival to the daycare.

When we got to the room, we were greeted by a kind, beautiful soul who cared for my child daily. She sweetly offered as I handed her his clothes, "Oh, we'll get him dressed."

Oh, HAIL NO!

I (sweetly), through gritted teeth, responded. "No, you won't. HE will."

And the result of this?

Charlie never left the house in his pajamas again.
The three-year-old version of short-term pain/long term gain.
Keep this in mind.

How to Set Limits, Options A to D

A – Best: Allowing space for the hysteria that can occur when we set limits, can be, and often is, "perfect" parenting. It can be used for success on your end. It takes courage in the face of the madness to allow it to do its good work, like allowing Charlie to have his meltdown over his own decision. Execute these magical steps:

1. Empathize. Make the child feel heard and understood.
2. State the limit clearly with no BUT at the start of the sentence.
3. Give the person options/choices to meet their need of power since they have no power over step number two.

B - Good: Feeling like a deer in the headlights? If you can't think of anything to say in the moment when all hell's breaking loose, simply repeat what the child said. Be a parrot. "You don't want to get dressed." "You don't want to go to bed." "You would like a cookie."

C - Do no harm: Walk away, zip your lips, say less. Let him have a tantrum. Don't try to appease him.

D - Harm: You know what this is by now. Don't do this.

Stay away from option D and you will be a perfEct parent.

THREE

The Relentless Broken Record

At any point in the day, we parents are often bombarded with the relentless verbal broken record in the form of your child's persistent line of questioning. It sounds like this: "Are we there yet? Are we there yet? Are we there yet?" Or, "I want some juice. I want some juice. I want some juice." Maybe you've heard this one, "Why can't I?" And a few moments later, "Why can't I?"

You get the idea.

Maybe it has even happened today! This nails-on-the-chalkboard type of communication from your "greatest good" can drive every sane parent crazy. Psychologists call it *perseveration*, an obsessive statement on repeat. Parents call it "shut the heck up." At its best, it is the child's attempt to wear us down till they get what they want. It can feel like an assault. And, the assault works.

We DO get worn down.

What *can* we do in the face of this repetitive verbal assault? When all else has failed, when you have responded with the easy-to-understand response any sane parent would, but still your child continues asking the same question, hoping for a different response from you? Then give it to him—a different response. There is one simple response that almost always diffuses the situation on both sides.

It involves love.
Respond with love.
Respond with "I love you."

•••

WHEN MY KIDS WERE LITTLE, we would make this thirteen-hour car ride a few times a year. That's a whole lot of time to expect little people to entertain themselves in a confined space! We would even make "state" bags, an idea my sister conjured up where whenever we crossed a state's border into a new state, the kids would open a little brown lunch bag full of distractions—I mean, fun things—trying to help them and us through the long ride. I had let the kids know we wouldn't be arriving until after dinner. Charlie began the questioning and we were still in the morning hours before lunch!

Charlie: When are we going to be there?
Me: When ARE we going to be there?
Charlie: After dinner.
Me: Right. Have we had lunch?
Charlie: No.
And then it kept coming...
Charlie: Are we there yet?
Me: I love you, Charlie.
Charlie: Are we?
Me: I love you, Charlie.
LOVE.

It helped me in those moments of tension to access the love I have for him. It softened me and it softened him. He smiled, too.

Answer them *once*, and then the ongoing response from you should be a soft, "I love you."

Maybe the message comes with a warm smile?

You might even get one back from your child. He can keep asking and you can keep responding. Not to their question—which has already been answered—but to extend love verbally to them.

It works.

It really works.

Give it a try and let the magic unfold.

I love you.

I love you.

I loooooove you (convincing yourself and your child the more it comes out of your mouth).

How to Deal with the Broken Record, Options A to D

A - Ideal: Answer the question one time and follow up with "I love you, Charlie."

B - Good: Respond one time and answer their question, "After lunch." Know that ignoring them can escalate their attempts to get you to give them attention.

C - Do no harm: Repeatedly answer your child, "After lunch, after lunch, after lunch…"

D - Harm: Shaming the child for asking over and over (are you deaf?), yelling responses back to him (I told you, not yet!), losing control of yourself and your emotions while driving (Stop asking me that!).

Note: Safety is the main job of the driver. Keep your focus on that. More on driving and fighting/yelling in the car in the next chapter.

Stay away from option D and you will be a perfEct parent.

FOUR

The Car Ride

The daily shuttle that occurs across America every day can be filled with tension. Driving is hard enough to do without the onslaught of infighting among the natives in the backseat. Or the "touching" complaints that arise from the back seat with expectations that Mom or Dad, driving the huge weapon that a car truly is, can somehow also manage to address the issue while at the wheel.

Car rides/driving with kids can be daunting.

The fighting? One Option A is to say nothing and pull the car over (to a safe spot). Calmly wait there until the battle subsides and when it does, begin driving again. If fighting continues, pull over again.

This works best when the children are invested in getting to their destination, and you have the time to delay getting where you're going.

Obviously, you might not be able to do this at certain times, but when you *are* able to pull over, see what happens. They often become curious as to "Why are we on the side of the road?" Or, "Why are we sitting in this parking lot?"

Less is more here.

No words.

No yelling.

No lecturing.

No begging on your end.

Just peace and patience until the fighting subsides. Deep breathing works in the interim. Maybe even earbuds with your current favorite song or podcast could give you a needed reprieve while you are waiting. The point is not to buckle and get involved with their spat. Simply wait it out.

Remember: We're each 100 percent responsible for what we say and what we do...no matter what is done or said to us—100 percent responsible.

Not 80 percent responsible.

Not 60 percent responsible.

Totally 100% responsible.

> We are 100 percent responsible for what we say and what we do... not 80 percent responsible... not 60 percent responsible.

We may have been told or taught that if someone hits us, we're entitled to hit them back (the eye for an eye concept). Or, if someone yells at us, we're justified in yelling back at them.

Consider, instead, being 100 percent responsible for what you say and do. If someone hits you and you choose to hit them back, you're responsible for that. If someone yells at you and you decide to yell back at them, you are responsible for that.

So, when our kids are pushing and pushing our trigger buttons (and they learn *exactly* how best to do that), we remain responsible for our reactions and our responses.

One-hundred percent.

•••

GRACE WAS FIVE, CHARLIE WAS THREE and my niece Cecilia was two. I had her for a week while my sister and her husband took Eberle, her sister, to Disneyland. That was the week I purchased the $1.79 hook and eye latch from the hardware store for the bedroom door.

For the *inside of the door. My bedroom door.*

WHY?

Because I'm 100 percent responsible for what I say and what I do, no matter what is done to me.

Three kids under five tested me.

At one point I chose to lock myself into the bedroom to give myself space and time to calm down. Just on the other side of that door I could hear three small children melting down.

I was feeling within me the possibility of D erupting.

I did C. Do no harm.

I removed myself briefly from the situation so I could regroup and calm myself. D could have easily occurred if I was on the other side of the door. I definitely was going to do or say some things I likely would regret. But I had the power to prevent that. I chose C.

Simply stay away from Option D and you're a perfEct parent.

But, what do we do when difficult situations occur in the confined spaces of a car? What if they're interrupting your adult conversation going on in the front seat? What's the right (and safe) way to handle it? We DO have to maintain our focus on the road, after all!

Don't take your eyes off the road and don't stop your conversation. Instead, if you're able, reach a hand to the backseat and rub a leg, hold a hand, or rub a knee of whomever is seeking attention. This sends a message to the child that they're being heard. And, they're going to have to wait until there's a pause in the conversation.

It works.

The belief that the child has in that moment is **attention = love**. A gentle touch reminds them they are loved and important to you. But do not give in to their interruption, allowing them to divert your conversation.

Don't address them and turn around to look at them. Any words or eye contact you give them during the interrupting is like paying them money to keep interrupting. It's positive reinforcement for negative behavior we do not want to encourage in them.

By simply giving them a gentle touch, you are giving them the attention they need, without reinforcing their interrupting. This gentle attention feeds them with love. When a child interrupts you, they are checking in with you at those very times when you're focused elsewhere (e.g., driving and conversing with another adult, on the phone, after you've put them to bed, in the middle of the night when you're asleep), subconsciously wondering if they are *still* important to you, reaching out to find the answer.

Now, let's look at a different piece of the encapsulated car ride that we find maddening: the FLAT conversation that universally occurs after school between parents and kids:

"How was school?"

"Fine."

"What did you do?"

"Nothing."

"What did you learn?"

"Nothing."

Maddening?

Yes.

You are not alone.

As I said, it is a universal conversation.

Let's explore this a bit.

When you arrive home from working (whatever form that might take), how chatty are you? Do you need time to transition? Relax? Decompress? Introverts especially need this. Introversion versus extroversion is not about sociability or friendliness. Rather, it's about how we recharge our batteries.

Do we get energy by being around people or do we recharge by being in solitude? Introverts (who are roughly 30 percent of the population) need to recharge with downtime. They're the ones who are the least chatty after being in an environment all day that's usually designed for extroverts. Our American culture prizes extroversion. (The opposite is true in the Asian cultures where introversion is valued.) An insightful book on the topic is by Susan Cain, *Quiet*. She has a fabulous TED talk on the subject as well.

So during the after-school car ride or reentry into the home, a child can feel like they're being interrogated, complete with the hot spotlight searing down on them.

How was school?

What did you do today?

What did you learn?

So, think about a different approach. Option A might be to *dialogue* about *your* day. A dialogue involves two people. It is an *exchange* of information. Talk about what you've been doing. Share. Dialoguing might sound like this...

"Hey bud, great to see you. How did math go today?"

"Fine."

"Oh, good." [pause] "Today I had lunch with Aunt Gretchen. She has started working for a local farmer and drives a combine. She's even learning to drive a semi!" [pause] "I saw clients today and Rose [the family dog] and I went on an awesome walk. She seemed so happy to be out of the house!"

This is where you might be surprised at what they begin to volunteer. *Maybe* they offer nothing, but *maybe* they begin to share. Regardless, you've given them an offering of a dialogue: a *mutual* sharing of information. You're sharing the intimacy of your day-to-day life. It feels so much better than interrogation to a child. And, they get to know you better too! They hear about the fullness of you. Your humanity. And, they realize you actually *do* things in the day in-between seeing them off to school and picking them up after school. You have a life of activity...just like they do. Consider sharing some of that and see where the conversation leads then. It might have two sides instead of one!

•••

THIS PROBABLY WON'T WIN ME ANY Mother of the Year awards. Here goes anyway.

When there was screaming or fighting in the car and there was no opportunity or time to pull over? Option B for me was rolling down the windows. Rain, snow, sleet or shine.

For real.

Allow me to explain.

I had shared with them previously that it's my job, first and foremost as driver of the car, to keep the passengers safe. That's my job. And, to make all these decisions up here and watch all the other drivers, lights, pedestrians, signs, etc., it takes *a lot of my attention and focus* to keep tabs on what is happening OUTSIDE the car. At the same time, yelling, screaming, and fighting also took my attention and energy to help INSIDE the car. So what they could expect going forward is that, in those times when I need my energy to keep us safe and they're fighting, they will see their windows go down so they can get out whatever it is they need to get out. Scream it out. Let it out of the car. Release it all. And, when they've gotten it all out, it will be obvious as it will most certainly be quieter and calmer inside the car. Then I'll put the windows back up.

So they can be doing their noisy fighting thing, and without any words coming out of my mouth, the windows will go down.

They were often a bit surprised.

They often found it a bit inconvenient (snowy days especially).

And it was quite effective.

Mother of the Year.

How to Handle the Out-of-Control Car Ride, Option A to D

A - Ideal: When there is **bickering/touching/fighting** in the car, pull over and say nothing. Begin driving the weapon (car) again when there is an intermission to the antics in the back seat. If it starts again, pull over. Say nothing and master your deep breathing. Maybe even plug in your earbuds for some soothing music. Safety is your highest priority here. If you are rattled, pull over and take care of yourself and the safety of those kids you love so dearly. Less is more here.

Mothers of the Year? She rolls down the windows.

Interrupting? Reach back and touch lovingly in some way. (I found myself often rubbing a leg gently while driving). Then, after you're done with your adult conversation, verbally acknowledge them for their patience, even though they might not have been patient, and listen to whatever it is they wanted to share. Remember, this isn't about whatever it is they're saying. It's about them wanting to know they're valued and loved by you in that moment.

Attention = love.

Children just want confirmation. A loving touch provides that confirmation. Key word there is *loving*. I've found it challenging to demonstrate love when I'm annoyed and irritated. Our challenge here is to do just that—if it's not loving, then the child will not wait patiently.

Radio silence in the car after school? Dialogue with them about your day. Let it be a two-way street rather than turning on the heat of the interrogation lamp. When we can *converse* rather than interrogate, we might just get what we want: a *conversation!*

B - Good: Whether it's fighting, interrupting or silence you're dealing with, a good B solution is to be curious and ask gentle questions while letting go of the outcome and what information might be coming back. Allow room for silence. With fighting, silence is golden as well on your end.

C - Do no harm: After you get in the car and there's silence, greet them, then say nothing else and see what happens. Allow for silence. They may pick up the ball and begin a conversation. If there's fighting, listen to your own music or earphones, knowing that safety and your state of calm is in *everyone's best interest* as you drive the car.

D - Harm: Allowing the stress of the misbehavior occurring inside of the car to cause some kind of accident. Complaining that they never share, shaming them, or yelling at them.

Stay away from option D and you will be a perfEct parent.

FIVE

Hitting, Biting, Calling Names

Hopefully you haven't had this happen to you, but many of us have: hitting. If you haven't, lucky you. Out of frustration, disappointment, or anger, a child can lash out aggressively in a physical manner at the people he is safest with, the parent. Not only hitting, but biting and name calling can be a part of this aggressive package.

Each of us has a right to safety, especially physical safety. The natural tendency or reaction when our child lashes out physically is to do something in retaliation—bite back, hit back, lash out verbally—punish in some way.

This is revenge.

The revenge cycle is one of hurt. I feel hurt, so I am going to hurt you back.

Hurt people hurt people.

Try to resist this natural reaction. Override your instincts. Be the mature one. Even sending them to their room can backfire. It can turn into a power struggle trying to get them to go there. "Yes, you will," followed by "No, I won't." And, this is added on *top* of whatever it was that initially caused them to hit or bite in the first place.

There is a simple solution to this.

Move.

Yes, you move. The adults?

Yes.

Why? Because *we* are more resourced in this moment than the child. We can try to rationally protect ourselves and state calmly that we need to leave the room, "I don't want to be hurt." So, we can go to a nearby room, even if it's a wide-open doorframe to the next room.

Move.

The very important message we are sending our child is, "I will protect myself from harm." If the child follows you to the next room, summon up your gentle/calm face, kneel down at their eye level and ask, "Are you all done hitting (or biting or calling me names)?" It is at this moment when you will be looked at like you're an alien.

The child will have NO idea what you mean. That was *so* thirty seconds ago.

If they respond affirmatively, yes, they are done hitting (or biting or calling names), then stay in the same room with them. If not, move to another room.

Same message.

"I will not allow myself to be subject to pain or insults from you. I have power over that. I can choose to protect myself without imposing anything on you."

So many parents report the child will not leave them alone. In that case, you certainly can resort to locking yourself in a bathroom or bedroom—so long as you know the child is safe (which they usually are). In these cases of physical and verbal attacks, the adult is the one needing safety. It is self-preservation and the message is strong, "I will not allow myself to be harmed by you." When your child is calm and/or done feeling angry, share space with them again. In essence, you are making yourself a privilege for them to be around.

Which you are.

You're setting a boundary.

The migration out of the room needs to include anyone else in the room as well. All siblings, babies, dog, **everyone**—leave the room. Leave the abuse.

The message is loud and clear that no one wants to be around someone who injures them.

We can keep ourselves safe from any harm.

The beauty of this intervention is that it is 100 percent within your control. You don't need to get the child to do anything. In fact, they don't even need to stop biting, hitting, or calling names. They can continue doing so. It's simply that no one will be around to let them do that to their bodies (or ears). We each have that right. We each can protect ourselves. We have power over that.

Keeping in mind that we are 100 percent responsible for what we say and do at all times, this exodus from the room where the violator is sends that message loud and clear.

We are 100 percent responsible.

Your partner is 100 percent responsibility for their words and actions.

Your children are 100 percent responsible for their words and actions.

Regardless of what is said or done to me, I am responsible for my choice at all times. If I am hit and I hit back, I am responsible. If I am yelled at and I yell back, I am responsible—100 percent.

Remember the hook and eye latch I bought for the bedroom door? It is C, do no harm. Whatever I might say or do on the other side of the door is far worse than locking myself inside to regroup/self-calm. I did not want to do harm with my words or my actions.

I calmed myself and then was able to conduct myself in a way I wouldn't regret once I emerged.

DO NO HARM is fabulous parenting.

How to Deal with Hitting, Biting, Calling Names, Option A to D

A - Ideal: Should you find yourself on the receiving end of any **physical harm** (hitting, biting) or **verbal insults**. We need to remove ourselves and anyone else from the situation.

The instinct is to move the child. However, they are already out of control, upset, agitated. And in that state, it's very hard to receive direction. Isn't it the same for you when you're out of control or upset?

So, what we *can* do is we can move ourselves.

First, move across the room or to the next room and see if that helps. When the child follows and approaches you, bend down and ask if they are done hitting/biting/calling you names. If they say yes, stay in proximity to them. If they continue to hit/bite/ name call, move to the next room. This can be done ultimately in a bathroom or bedroom behind closed doors where the child may very well be conducting "the perfect fit" outside the door. This is much preferred to whatever you might be saying or doing if the door was open. A very strong message is being sent, "I will not tolerate being harmed." And what fabulous modeling *that* is! Calm yourself and then join when safe to do so. If the child hits again, continue in this manner. One client had such horrible assault occurring from child to parent that it took three weeks for the message to truly sink in. It may get worse or intensify before it gets better.

It did for them.

It *will* work.

Stick with it.

B - Good: Give them something to hit or bite, like a stuffed animal or doll, instead of a person. Invite them to go into the potty for name calling/potty words. Those words hurt our ears and that's the only appropriate place for potty words. Give them free reign to unleash their potty words there in the bathroom with the door closed. Knock yourself out. Come out when you've said all you need to say.

C - Do no harm: Walk away, breathe, tend to yourself.

D - Harm: Hitting the child back, biting them back, eye for an eye, calling them names.

Stay away from option D and you will be a perfEct parent.

SIX

Staying Seated at Dinner...How to Glue Them to Their Chairs and Other Mealtime Challenges...

Well, this is an easy chapter.

Super glue.

They use it now to glue skin together—why not children to seats?

Let's assume you're out of super glue and really want dinner time to be people *seated* around a table. First, let's consider your child's attention span. What is realistic to expect? I'm not so much tied to age as I am to considering individual children. A girl of three may be able to sit still a whole lot longer than a boy of five. It varies. So please consider what is a realistic expectation for each child. Ten minutes might feel like a lifetime to some kids.

•••

WITH TWO KIDS UNDER FOUR, it took us many experiences in restaurants to realize we no longer wanted to be doing this. But before we came to that decision, we tried many a strategy and the following are some of the successful ones. Keep in mind, we still gave it up eventually. These are offered for when you're brave enough or simply required to dine in a restaurant with kids.

First of all, we always scoped out the dining room for any booths. That way, Sean could sit on the outside of one of the benches, containing one kid in the playground of the bench seat, and I could sit on the outside of the other bench of the booth. Containment.

We were sentries.

Then, we would order as fast as humanly possible.

No dallying here.

After about five to seven minutes of booth "fun", then came the field trip.

To the bathroom.

Yep! Who knew how much fun bathrooms can be? There is so much to do there! There's water, and loud sounds of flushing, and people, and doors, and loud wind that blows! How fun is that?

And, it's a destination available in every restaurant. A whole new adventure to explore.

Every restaurant bathroom definitely had our germs in it.

After that extended field trip, we could expect at least another five minutes of attention span. If really lucky, maybe ten minutes. In this time, hopefully, the food would come.

And then there was *that* fun to have.

If the mood by now was tanking for one child, then one of us would now be walking the restaurant with one child (or two), while the other adult was trying to eat their meal. Then, we would pass the baton to the other and give them an opportunity to eat their now slightly cold food while the other would take the kids outside on the sidewalk and have them run to the pole and back three times.

And, we are paying for this experience?

How often do y'all want to do this with your kids?

We gave it up. It just wasn't worth it.

Dining out, for me, is meant to be civilized. Pleasant. Relaxing. I enjoy being served. I enjoy exploring foods and places. I enjoy not doing the dishes. It is a pleasure.

This experience with my children was not that.

Let's touch on ordering for children. Since my children could talk, I have never ordered for them.

They can talk.

They can order.

For me, it was a wonderful opportunity for them to speak to authority figures beyond their parents. They could state their needs to other adults. And have us there to support them.

●●●

THIS MEMORY IS STILL KIND OF heartbreaking for me. Charlie was six and asked us to go to Steak and Shake. It's a chain in the Midwest that has kid-friendly food. And booths. So, here we are at the place where *he* had requested. The server came, the three of us placed our orders. Charlie said nothing to her. What he was saying (to us) was that he wanted me to order for him. I encouraged him to order for himself. He stayed silent. The gal left with our orders. She came back once to check in on us and I shared with Charlie that he could tell her what he wanted now and that this would likely be his last opportunity.

He said nothing.

The food came.

We ate.

Charlie did not.

Heartbreaking, huh? I still feel it.

The good news? It never happened again.

Short-term pain, long-term gain.

I can report that Charlie has successfully ordered for himself since!

Back to dinner in the safe confines of your home. Consider introducing a timer. Let the kids know your expectations ahead of time (so respectful). For example, maybe they must stay seated for ten minutes, and then consequences if they get up. "If you get up from the table, it looks to me like you're finished eating. I will assume you are and I'll put the food away." So, you have communicated that you expect them to stay seated on their bottoms for ten minutes and eat their food. Set the timer for ten minutes. You've been clear what their getting up from the table is communicating to you. Now what?

Whenever a limit is set, expect for it to be tested. If it isn't, be pleasantly surprised.

> Whenever a limit is set, expect for it to be tested.
> If it isn't, be pleasantly surprised.

This is worth repeating: Expect for a limit to be tested; if not, be pleasantly surprised.

It's their job to see if we mean it.

So, they get up.

It's your job now to remove their plate and take the contents to the sink, trash or disposal.

Ouch! Harsh?

We're going for firm *and* kind here.

This is the firm part.

The kind part came earlier.

You shopped for the food, bought the food, and made them dinner.

And, you have courteously set the expectation ahead of time.

How many times have your children eaten next to nothing at a meal and survived?

They will survive this one too.

My intention throughout these strategies is to provide long-term benefit. It may very well feel like short-term pain for long-term gain. Often, as parents, we try to get the immediate situation under control and give less consideration to what the child might be retaining from this interaction for tomorrow or next week. We are keeping the long-term in mind here. When they get up, they communicate they're done. We simply follow through with the message they are sending us: they are finished eating.

•••

When Grace was little, she had some wild and crazy curly hair with no bangs. And, I mean wild. (I also have naturally curly hair.) We had a hard time convincing her to keep it out of her face. She'd run around with it loose, getting it all tangled, and then I'd have the unpleasant task of trying to comb it out. So, naturally I wanted her to wear her hair up to keep it under control and out of her eyes. The name we gave to anything that went into her hair to keep it pulled back was "hair-ups." They kept the hair "up." They would be put in the hair and sometimes she'd take them out. Whenever she took out the "hair-up" and the hair was floundering around in her face, I let her know she was communicating that she was ready for bed: nap or nighttime.

That solved the problem: Hair down in the face communicated bedtime. Grace didn't want to go to bed. Hair would voluntarily go up again, out of the face.

That's the same message we're communicating about meal-time. She understood that when she got up from dining, she was communicating something. She's communicating that she's through eating. We removed the food. Naturally, she sometimes was hungry later.

How will you handle that? At our house, a banana was always available. Don't save them from being hungry by being a short-order cook. You did your part. You earned money for the food, you shopped for the food, you prepared the food.

Dinner is dinner.

Not having other food is a natural consequence of choosing not to eat. Saving them from natural consequences prolongs the learning. It is effective learning. It is how *we* learn.

We speed, we get a ticket.

We don't wear a coat, we get cold.

We don't eat, we feel hungry.

What about when they complain about food? At home? At friend's houses? At Grandma's?

Teach them to say nothing and simply leave it there on the plate. Problem solved. If asked by adults, they can then offer, "I don't care for that."

Simple courtesy.

•••

THIS REMEDY OF "I DON'T CARE FOR THAT" was SO needed at our house. Prior to that, food would be prepared and then the kids (mostly one in particular) felt free to offer their dramatic editorial on what was placed in front of them. I often prepared it, and cooking not being my thing in general, this felt rather discouraging. While simple, the meals I prepared showed my attention to health and balance. And, who can make a meal every night where *every* person likes *all* the parts?

Not me.

So the complaining would really get to me. And, it was often somewhat dramatic. My daughter was known for this line: "Oh, this looks yucky. I can taste it with my eyes."

I remember these feedback sessions growing up too! My poor mom. First, she was a really good cook (which I am not). She was kind and generous enough to get up each morning and head down the stairs to make us ungrateful children breakfast every single day.

Every. Single. Day.

And, I mean a warm breakfast! Pancakes, French toast, oatmeal, Cream of Wheat, coffee cake, pecan rolls, scrambled eggs, poached eggs. Those are the highlights I remember. And, what did she get most mornings as she slowly walked down the stairs to prepare this for us? She would get loads of conflicting suggestions about what she should make for us. And those requests were different for different kids. It must have been so disheartening for her. I still don't know how she didn't go on strike.

We did not deserve her generosity.

To this day, I can still remember our picky little demands... my sister liked Cream of Wheat, I liked oatmeal. Me? French toast. Her? Pancakes. We were never satisfied. And my poor brother? I'm not sure he ever really got a vote. That's okay, though, because the family still jokes about how all the wrongs inflicted on him by having two older sisters got made up for by his daily trips to Dairy Queen after half-day kindergarten.

Every. Single. Day.

Finally, let's touch on taste buds. Apparently, kids have about twice the number of taste buds as adults do! No wonder they react so intensely to foods. And, why they tend toward bland, safe, repetitive foods. It's our job, however, to continue to expose them to new foods. It will take many exposures before a child warms up to a certain food…think seven to ten times. So, keep putting the lone strawberry on the plate. Keep setting out the piece of broccoli. Keep serving the hummus.

Expose. Expose. Expose. The natural resistance will wear down eventually.

How to Handle Mealtime Challenges, Option A to D

A - Ideal: Be realistic and set the expectations of time at the table, in the seat. Set a timer. (For small children, Timetimer.com gives them a visual and quantifies time, and iPads have some of these visuals as well.)

When they choose to get up, calmly take the food, letting them know they're telling you by getting up that they're finished eating. Keep in mind, firm *and* kind would be to take the food away and even place it in the trash or sink. We are *always* looking for the firm *and* kind option. No short-order cooking for them later. Clearly outline what is, and is not, available to them later. (Yogurt or a banana, etc.)

Teach them to say, "I don't care for that." Or to say nothing if they're not interested in trying the food. It's okay for them to not like certain foods. We all have different palates. Forcing a child to eat food when they are not hungry or don't care for it conditions them to override their own knowing/intuition about their own body and the messages that it sends about hunger and fullness. They need to begin to tune in to that. And the messages we send

about food can promote or inhibit that learning. Their relationship with food is important. Coaching them about healthy foods,
sugary foods, and the energy each provides is important learning
for them.

B - Good: Observe them. "Seems like it's hard for you stay seated tonight." Or "Looks like you have some moves you need to make
before you can eat?" or "Looks like you're not hungry right now."
And make every effort to enjoy your own meal with whomever
remains there with you.

C - Do no harm: Ignore the getting up, not coming back, and
continue enjoying your own food and company.

D - Harm: Making them sit at the table until they eat all their
food (can promote eating disorders). Comparing them to a sibling
who does sit still or eats diverse foods. Shaming or yelling at them.

Stay away from option D and you will be a perfEct parent.

SEVEN

Interrupting

Trying to have a conversation in the company of small children seems like a simple desire. Why is it so difficult?

It's difficult because children equate attention to love.

Attention = love, remember?

Any attention your child receives will feel like love. This means negative attention too! Yelling at them or lecturing them even qualifies to some degree. Consider it like money—any time a child is given negative attention, it's like paying them to repeat the very same behavior since they're being "loved" for it. You're rewarding them for their inappropriate behavior.

What do we do when the interrupting happens in the day-to-day activities of life?

Attention = LOVE

Ignoring them often causes them to escalate the attention-seeking behavior. They get louder and louder and more dramatic in their attempts to secure our attention. This is due to the belief they harbor: "I'm only loved if I have your attention." Your child needs to know they're loved by you even when you're talking to someone else or talking on the phone.

How do we do that?

Our monumental task is to *love* them *and,* at the same time, not pay (or reward) them to keep interrupting. We achieve this by loving them with no words and no eye contact.

If we look at them or say any words to them, we have paid the child to repeat the behavior. Instead, make physical contact while continuing the conversation or activity they've tried to interrupt. Touch their hand, hold their hand, rub their arm, stroke their hair, pull them in to you, rub their back. Do whatever gentle touch they find receptive and loving. When you're in the car and they're in the back seat attempting to interrupt, gently rub their leg. This loving contact is meant to communicate to your child their importance to you while not stopping your conversation. It's meant to hold them off *only* until there is a natural pause in the conversation when you might then turn to your child and say, "Thank you for waiting. What is it you wanted to tell me?" Or, "Thank you for your patience" (even if they demonstrated very little to no patience). Acknowledge them and then provide your undivided attention. The attention is given *when it is appropriate.* No attention is given when they're trying to interrupt.

After many, many physical demonstrations of love, Grace and Charlie eventually began to stand next to me while I was on the phone, waiting patiently. They both began to trust that I would attend to them when the timing worked. I have a friend whose youngest daughter will hold her pinky while she is talking, waiting for her mom to finish. She knows she will be attended to soon and no longer feels the need to interrupt. Trust has been built.

In the heat of situations when a child is interrupting, this non-verbal form of love is SO much harder to deliver than it sounds. I found it difficult to demonstrate love when feeling annoyed and irritated. Actually, love might be the furthest feeling in that particular moment. The tendency, then, is for the touch/affection that is given to harbor much of that annoyance and frustration. If that is the case, your child will not stop trying to get your attention.

IT MUST BE GENUINE LOVE.

When we're annoyed and irritated, the most natural form of touch is patting. Patting? Yep. Patting. Why? It feels like a dog—a bit demeaning. Patting to a child does not feel loving. When I have role-played this over the years with my clients, and I'm playing the role of the annoying child, I ask the parent to nonverbally send love to me and to please not pat me. It usually begins with them holding my hand. I don't stop trying to get their attention. Then, they put their arm around me and often begin to pat me even though I had just reminded them not to pat. It's so natural to do. Our annoyance and irritation travel down our arm and out our hand in an annoyed and irritated way.

So, it must be very intentional to truly be physically *loving* to our child. For the role play, I'm on my knees trying to get the attention of my "parent" and they're in a chair when we demonstrate this. When they pull me in to them in a genuinely loving way, I stop trying to get their attention.

Why? Because it feels like I have *some* of their attention *and* I feel loved. It's not the full meal deal of attention I was originally looking for, but it's enough. I feel they love and care about me by their actions.

When we demonstrate the role play with *me* being the parent and *the client* playing the interrupting child, sometimes the adult does not stop trying to get my attention until they're in my lap and I'm affectionately rubbing their back or arm.

It works.

Love works every time.

This method of handling a child interrupting is the same remedy you would use when they're trying to get your attention at other inappropriate times. One of these is after you have put them to bed. If (or when) they choose to get out of bed, do not look at them, do not talk to them—gently turn them around and with gentle pressure on the shoulders, redirect them back to bed. You may even tuck them in (remember we are trying to be loving here) and then leave. You don't want to overpower a child by carrying them back to bed if they walked themselves out of bed. If they walked themselves out, then they're capable of walking themselves back. If you need to "marionette" them by placing the cups of your hands under their armpits (for the collapsers), then do so—but do so lovingly and even playfully. If you have a child who consistently gets out of bed, the first night of this method might take thirty-five times of not looking at them, not talking to them and gently helping them walk back to bed. The second night will likely be eleven times and the third night might be three. It will taper because the child begins to understand the message: "I get nothing by getting out of bed. No one is yelling at me to get back into bed. No one is begging me to stay in bed. No one is coddling me. I get *nothing*."

That nothing will keep them in bed.

There are some things I can guarantee.

This is one of them.

It will taper each night. Hang in there. You can do this.

The same holds true for the middle of the night visits. Treat them the same as with bedtime infractions. Lovingly steer them back to bed. You're the best judge of whether your child is waking you because they're scared, sick, or if they're waking you out of habit. If there's a pattern, it is usually habit and you can feel safe to handle it in the above manner. But if they're scared or sick, there may be a different situation to address.

You decide.

What about when they crawl in bed with you in the middle of the night? Treat that the same as above (of course, someone has to wake up and be alert enough to do this):

No words.

No eye contact.

Gently walk them back to their bed.

Short-term pain, long-term gain.

Another maddening moment for parents is the moment it is time to leave the bedroom after the bedtime routine is complete. Before leaving the room and implementing this strategy, stand in the doorway of their room. Ask, "Is there anything else you want to say to me before I leave the room? When I leave, I won't be talking to you or looking at you anymore."

This is when the litany of chatter/requests erupts with, "Well, I need a drink. I need to go to the bathroom again. I'm hungry. I need a light. I need to tell you something," etc., etc.

How do you respond to their requests?

"Willing" needs to be a word in every parent's language.

It's different than "can" or "can't," "should" or "shouldn't."

Willing implies choice.

"I am willing to do that" or "I am not willing to do that." Just because they asked for it does not mean you are "willing" to do it.

> Just because they asked for it does not mean you are "willing" to do it.

And, you'll know when it's truly incorporated into the home when your children begin to use the word "willing." "Mom, I am not willing to do that," or "Mom, I *am willing to do that*."

Just smile when you hear that from them. It means you've modeled some beautiful language. Then, know that it's language that they will likely be using with their peers or partners or other authorities down the road! Success!

Expect that the child will get out of bed, despite you having set the expectations so very clearly.

Remember that whenever you set a limit, expect it to be tested. If not tested, be pleasantly surprised.

So, expect that your child is going to get out of bed. Be prepared for that. Assume it. Save yourself steps and wait outside the door!

Don't take it personally when they test limits. No lecture. Simply execute the plan. Calmly. No words, no eye contact. Over and over and over again until they get the message. And, sometimes it takes that. Three "overs"!

> Whenever you set a limit, expect it to be tested.
> If not tested, be pleasantly surprised.

•••

WHEN CHARLIE WAS THREE, HE LOVED to get out of bed. He was very curious about what was still happening downstairs. Night after night it happened. During this time, we had a family friend who would come over at night and do some bookkeeping for us in the office. Many nights after putting Charlie to bed, I would be sitting at my desk and she would be working at the other desk. Charlie would walk in (wearing the darling pajamas shorts with the dogs on them, blankie in hand) and curl up on the hardwood floor between us. All the while he had a look on his face that I called "eating his smile." He would be smiling and trying not to. He absolutely knew what he was doing. And, he was so freaking cute! Anyway, she knew she wasn't supposed to look at him or say anything to him. It was like having an elephant in the room. Right there. On the hardwood floor. In the middle of the space between us. It was SO hard not to "pay" him for his behavior by looking at this darling boy or talking to him. After she and I would finish our conversation, I would get up and go to him, gently put my hands under his armpits to pull him up, and guide him upstairs back to his bed.

No words.

No eye contact.

He would get tucked in and I would leave.

This often happened with him despite no "payment" to do so. The process of teaching him took many weeks of repetition.

Be prepared to do this *many* times, even on the first night. It will taper to less frequency the second night and even less the third night. Charlie maintained doing this little dance like it was a ritual for a while.

Heading into Option D… What does it feel like?

Remember the "dispassionate cop" goal? I mentally adopted that term as I was navigating the teen years. I had to remind myself over and over again. "Dispassionate" means no lecturing, no hysteria, no taking it personally, sticking with the facts *calmly.* The "cop" part is simply delivering the expectations and consequences due to *their* choice. It's hard for many of us to get to the "dispassionate" part. We're usually quite the opposite = impassioned!

After all, these are our KIDS and we are so emotional about them. It is natural. Instinctual. Biological.

And, we must find that place sometimes of dispassion in our delivery. Because calm is love. Patience is love.

•••

I WAS SIXTEEN WHEN MY DAD FOUND out I had purchased alcohol for my sister that day (who was older than me and also underage). He was a big fish in a little pond—a lawyer in a small town. He became very impassioned yelling at me—grabbing me, screaming in my face, and twisting my t-shirt so hard it ripped under the armpits while bending me back over his suburban.

My mom watched this "impassioned" event from the porch.

Naturally, out of love for me he was scared. And, that is not what came out of his mouth, however. In fact, that admission never came out. Rather, what came out at me was anger and fury. The only part of his impassioned lecture I did remember was the term "excise cops." I share this so it might help you understand or remember what it feels like as a child to have Option D happen to you. All I was thinking was *Dad, you need to get a grip. You are OUT OF CONTROL.* I was definitely NOT reflecting on my behavior as he had probably intended for me to do. I was not thinking, *Boy, I better not do this again.*

Here are some thoughts that I *did* have:

I better be sneakier next time, so I don't have to deal with THIS again.

Man, he's out of control.

I just want to run away. (retreat)

I want to get even with him. (revenge)

Why did mom just stand there? (felt like betrayal)

I hate him.

He must have had a bad day.

Notice, nowhere in these thoughts am I thinking what he was hoping or intending I would be thinking after his impassioned delivery. I trust he was hoping I'd be thinking some version of:

Man, that was stupid. I better not do that again.

I did not think that.

Not once.

However, if he could have calmly (dispassionate cop) sat me down and told me he was very upset, angry, scared for me due to the fact that I purchased alcohol underage, and educated me with information about who excise cops are, that they sometimes hang out around liquor stores, that legally here are the consequences of what can happen to me, and that he loves me and was so very worried about me.

What would have happened then?

I likely would have let his message in.

To my heart.

From his heart.

Who knows where my underage alcohol buying "career" would have gone then?

But D happened. The receiving end of D does not have desirable outcomes.

What was it like for you to be on the receiving end of physical harm?

Yelling?

Shaming?

Anger?

Humiliation?

Option D does not yield our intended result.

It never has.

And, it is super hard to be a "dispassionate cop."
It takes practice.
You can do it.
You will.
You are worth it.
They are worth it.

How to Handle Interrupting, Option A to D

A - Ideal: Using no words and making no eye contact, reach out and touch the child to transmit love when they are trying to interrupt and/or get attention at an inappropriate time.

Attention equals love.

We, the parents, are attempting to give love but not the full attention until there is an appropriate break in the conversation—in person or on the phone.

B - Good: Give them a look while loving them, trying to buy time, while talking to someone on the phone or in person, pleading for them to wait or be patient. (Haven't we all been doing this for years anyway? Maybe not the loving them part?)

C - Do no harm: Give them your attention by interrupting what you're doing. In essence, this option would be like paying them to continue with the interrupting/attention-seeking behavior. This option might be harming you, however. You decide.

D - Harm: You get the idea here…any communication that hurts or shames the child—yelling at them to get back into bed or yelling for them to wait for you until you get off the phone. Funny here that we might be yelling at them to have patience, yet we are not demonstrating it! Remember that favorite quote about parenting?

"Who you are speaks so loudly I can't hear anything you're saying."

Our children are watching us. They're seeing what we *do*, not what we *say* to them. The old adage, "Do as I say, not as I do" does not really apply. They are sponges, absorbing all they see us model for them.

They are watching us.

Stay away from option D and you will be a perfEct parent.

EIGHT

Lying. What to Do?

It seems almost unbelievable your child would straight-up lie to your face. They act so innocent! The good news here is that it's normal for children to experiment with lying. Your little angel lying to you doesn't mean you're raising a psychopath. It simply means your kid is *normal* and *experimenting* with lying.

Kids are natural storytellers. They love story. They learn through story. So do we.

So, when they're lying, maybe use the term *storytelling* rather than *lying* or calling them a *liar*. It's softer and allows more space for their normal experimentation here without them being harshly labeled.

> It's normal for children to experiment with lying.

They can get out of the corner this way.

So, they've told you a "story." How to deal with it? Most of the time, "stories" can be verified.

Lead with that.

"If I asked your sister/grandma/the teacher/friend if your story is true/what really happened, what would they say?" You're giving your child an opportunity to come clean. We want to give them as many opportunities to tell the truth as possible. We don't want to back them into a corner so they might feel the need to defend their lie.

Instead, you've given them an opportunity to be honest before you check into their story. They often 'fess up here as they know someone else can confirm or deny their story. If they still stand behind their story, then check in with the witnesses. You might also offer one last, "Anything else you want to tell me before I call Grandma?" Sometimes that's the nudge they need to spill the beans. If not, do your research and gather the facts.

If they are caught in a lie, then explain that the consequences of "telling stories" is a lack of trust. "It's hard for me to know when you're telling me a story or when you're telling me what really happened. It makes me feel confused and I have to make a choice between the story you're telling and what I'm hearing from Grandma." Feign a WHOLE lot of confusion and let them know, this is the consequence of telling stories that aren't true. They lose credibility. They are no longer believable in their words. Trust in their words is eroded.

Remember, not a big lecture here. Simply the facts. Dispassionate cop.

Now, for the remedy.

Next time you ask them a question where you KNOW the answer that they give you is true and honest, feign *confusion*.

For instance, you're in a fast food drive-thru and you ask if they would like a cheeseburger or chicken nuggets? They say chicken nuggets. You answer, "Since you sometimes tell stories, I'm confused right now if this might be one of those times you're telling me a story, so I'm going to go ahead and order you a cheeseburger."

And there it is. The consequence of lying.

Their words are not believed.

And, the reactions come quickly: "NO, I want nuggets!"

The "perfect fit" here is a good thing. They're feeling the consequences of *their* choice. It is highly effective. Same goes at home if you ask them if they would prefer spaghetti for dinner or hot dogs? They answer hot dogs. Feign confusion and explain that you'll be serving spaghetti since you can't tell if this is one of those times that they're telling a story or the truth.

The lying will diminish.

It diminishes as the child is forced to live in the consequences of their own actions. They *feel* the accountability of their own choice. It becomes *their* problem to rebuild *their* own credibility and accept the consequences of losing their credibility. It is through this felt sense that behaviors are likely to change.

How to Deal with Lying, Options A to D

A - Ideal: Ask if there's anything else they want to tell you before you confirm (or deny) their "story" with a witness (sibling, teacher, relative). Give them opportunities to come clean, all the while using the terms "story" and "storyteller" rather than "lie" and "liar." If they don't reveal more information, research their story with any available sources. Then, explain that one consequence of telling stories is that trust has been compromised/ broken. When that happens, it is confusing on the receiving end as we do not know when we're being told a story and when we're being told the truth; it's very hard for us to sort through. Then, when the time is right, (meaning that you KNOW they're telling the truth), feign confusion and make a decision the opposite way. The dinner option is to ask if they would like spaghetti or hot dogs that evening. If they choose hot dogs, explain that you'll be serving spaghetti as you are not sure if this is one of those times they're telling a story or telling the truth, since we're confused and have to "guess" what they really want.

Children (and adults) learn when we *must* face the consequences of our choices. When we feel the "ugh," the weight of our *own* choice is felt, and then *we might* be motivated to change. When we save children from the pain of the "ugh" moment, they have very little motivation to change. That's why children throwing a fit is sometimes a grand demonstration of their frustration with themselves and the situation—and possibly a precursor to change.

It's not always directed at us. They can be mad at themselves and it comes out at us.

And, this can be "perfect" parenting.

B - Good: Explore, investigate their story and try to find truth. Be a private investigator and try to get to the bottom of it.

C - Do no harm: Do nothing. Let the lie lie. See if it becomes a pattern.

D - Harm: Calling them a liar and telling them they can't be trusted. Shaming them. Yelling at them. Taking it personally, telling them they'll be a terrible adult, or threatening they'll end up in jail if they keep this up.

Remember, it's normal for kids to experiment with lying. Yet another developmental stage that they'll hopefully sail through!

Stay away from option D and you will be a perfEct parent.

NINE

Handing Things Over

At the start of the parenting class I've been teaching since our daughter was a toddler, the participants introduce themselves and share the names and ages of their children and one thing they're hoping to take away from the class. I do the same and share one thing I'm currently working on in regard to being a mom.

There was a gal years ago who introduced herself and then shared that what she *really* needed to leave this class with was to no longer dress her eight-year-old.

Her eight-year-old.

I guaranteed her that at the end of the five weeks, she would no longer be dressing her eight-year-old. And, she wasn't.

> We start out doing 100 percent
> of the tasks for our children.

We start out doing 100 percent of the tasks for our children. Those little lives are at our mercy. Literally, we feed them, clothe them, clean them, rock them to sleep, change their diapers. They don't even have to go to a toilet, sit in a chair, lift a finger to feed themselves. An infant is utterly dependent upon us for their every need. I believe the Universe designed it this way so we parents spend the first two years falling in love with our children and we spend the rest of their lives drawing upon that "in love" bank of goodness. My guess is that it keeps us from eating our young.

Thankfully this doesn't last forever. Gradually, infants begin to do small tasks for themselves. The Cheerios can make it to the mouth; the banana sometimes does too. They start to prop up their own bottle. After four months, they can put themselves to sleep (if we let them, so I am told). Then, they begin to learn mobility and we are no longer their full-time chariot. Eventually, around age three, they begin to put on their own clothes and can start washing their own hair around age five. As soon as they can talk, they can order for themselves at restaurants. They begin to open their own juice boxes, make their own lunch, sort the silverware from the dishwasher, RSVP to their own invitations, feed the dog, do the dishes. Around eleven, they can begin to do their own laundry. Kids learn to cook at all ages. Then, they begin to drive and earn their own money. Eventually, the idea is that we hand over all these tasks before they turn eighteen so that when they leave us, they're prepared for life and no longer depending on us for these tasks.

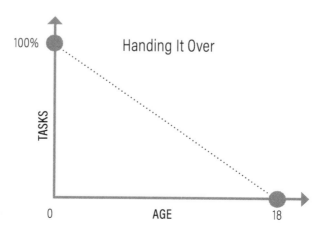

"What is one thing that I am doing for my child that
they could be doing for themselves?"

If we *keep* doing for them that which they can and should do for themselves, we're handicapping them. The child (or person) can then feel incapable. In adult terms outside of parenting, we call this *enabling*!

Parenting to protect *must* shift into parenting to prepare.

If we don't make that shift and *only* parent to protect, we're not preparing them.

It is our instinct to protect them. Mother bear and father bear instincts instruct us to spread our wings over them and protect them. We must override that instinct at each developmental stage and let them flail. Let them fail. Let them try. Let them get frustrated. Let them do it poorly. Let them forget their homework and lunch. Let them feel that breathtaking moment of "Ugh, I forgot it," or "Ahhh, this is so hard." When we allow them to feel their own mistakes, they then learn and can adjust their own choice for the future. Without that moment of "pain," there is little motivation to change. There's no growth.

Parenting to protect *must* shift into
parenting to prepare.

In the words of Barbara Colorosa, best-selling parenting author, "For every child who forgets, there is a parent who remembers."

So, if you have a forgetful child, perhaps you're being their memory and you don't realize it. That needs to stop. We must step out of the way, then, and make them responsible to remember things for themselves. This will be a bit of a shock for them when you decide to make a change. If you have been their memory and are no longer going to be doing that job, give them a heads-up. "Honey, tomorrow I won't be reminding you about the backpack (or the lunch). You'll need to remember yourself."

Now, this next part takes great self-control: DO NOT REMIND THEM WHEN YOU SEE THEM FORGETTING IT.

It is so very hard. But you've got to let them fail to help them grow.

We're hardwired to protect them from pain. See the homework, see the lunch, and say nothing. It is how they learn. When they do remember for themselves, they will feel capable, self-reliant, responsible, accountable. All good traits for those adults-in-training.

Natural consequences (saying nothing and not intervening) provide THE most effective learning. You are doing Option A when you do this.

Trust me on this.

It's short-term pain for long-term gain. If you continue being their memory, plan on budgeting for an apartment near them in college so you can wake them up in the morning to get to class on time and pack their books for them and the myriad of other responsibilities they have—they won't be remembering for themselves as they have depended on you to do everything for them.

Short-term pain.

Say nothing.

It works.

You've got to let them fail
to help them grow.

Really, I empathize with you how hard it is to say nothing and let the consequence speak for itself. I've been there. You want to save them from the pain. But the pain is what will teach them. We have to get out of the way and let them feel it. It's like learning to ride a bike. They'll fall a few times and skin their knees but eventually they'll learn.

Parenting to protect must shift to parenting to prepare, or we have not prepared them!

Natural consequences provide
THE most effective learning.

•••

WHEN GRACE WAS IN FIRST GRADE, I spent the first half of the year guiding her, showing her how to organize, asking her where she wanted to keep her backpack, folders, homework, etc. After the holiday break, I let Grace and her teachers know I would no longer be reminding her or helping with this. It was important for me to let the teachers know so they could take over being the authority and hold Grace accountable for doing her homework, remembering to turn it in, staying in from recess if needed to complete anything. She was a very typical first-born child and wanted to please, wanted to do it well, wanted to be responsible. And I stepped back anyway. The teachers had required reading nightly and had a daily progress chart that the child had to get a parent's signature on that they had completed the work. I stopped asking about it. So, there were some days she didn't progress if she had not done the task or gotten the proper documentation.

Of course, she was disappointed. And, it certainly shaped her choices that night about sharpening her focus on what she wanted and needed to remember.

It's so heartbreaking for us parents to watch our kids hurt or be disappointed. And, it's so vital that they experience these emotions while they have us by their sides. They learn they'll be okay when they feel disappointed. They'll be okay when they feel hurt. They have support.

The alternative is to protect these kids and work tirelessly so that they never experience disappointment or failure or pain. And what happens then?

Life will deliver it later. And they may not have you next to them to support them through it later. They might be on their own. Those would be foreign lands to navigate then.

Consider allowing them the opportunity to feel it all while they are under your roof.

Remember what I said about being a grandparent?

Can't wait!

I can't wait because I don't have to teach them these life skills of remembering, self-reliance, accountability, responsibility. I just get to indulge. Maybe I'll feel differently when I get to that point. Maybe I'll want to teach them life skills, but it's certainly not required of me then. Optional perhaps.

As parents, however, we do not have that choice.

We are tasked with grooming in them responsibility, honesty, accountability, self-reliance, and on and on. Short-term pain equals long-term gain. We want them going away from us at eighteen knowing how to cook a few things, how to manage money, how to remember a list of things they need to do, how to do their own laundry, how to recognize their own needs and have the confidence to meet them. They're never going to get to that place if we keep meeting these needs for them. We **must** hand them over.

> ## Short-term pain equals long-term gain.

So, when they're capable, stop feeding them. Stop ordering for them. (Remember Charlie in Steak and Shake?) Teach them how to wash their own hair and how many "over the head dumps" of the tiny bucket it takes to have clean hair. Allow them space to feed the dog. Give them the opportunity to pour their own drink (and fail sometimes). Let them forget their homework (or lunch) and know you're being an AMAZING parent when you let them forget it.

Firm AND kind. That's what we're looking for here.
Not firm OR kind.

Firm *and* kind lets them forget while giving them notice the night before that you're no longer going to be reminding/remembering for them. It's so hard to do and yields such beautiful results in your child.

> ## Firm AND kind.
> ## Not, firm OR kind.

A word on resistance.

You're going to get a lot of it. It's human nature.

If we can get someone else to do something for us rather than us do it, we let them. They're not just going to let go without a fight. So, make sure to give them a whole lot of encouragement through this process.

Here are some options:

"Boy, that does look hard. Give it a try."

"You can do it."

"Stay with it, you got this."

"Way to go for trying."

"Nice effort, bud."

Remind your child that our highest value is courage (trying). Success is not in the outcome being perfect, but in the effort that you tried. If you try and need help, I'm here for you. *That* is firm and kind.

Remember the gal at the end of the five weeks who was no longer dressing her daughter? We encouraged her *not* to be an audience to her child's resistance and to leave the room. Like her, just offer an encouraging statement, "You can do it" and then leave the room. Leave them with any task they've proven themselves capable of doing, e.g., getting dressed, making the bed, doing homework. Being an audience to them while they complain, whine, or beg is like adding fuel to the fire. That's because attention of any kind (positive OR negative) can fuel that need of feeling loved, important/valued/special since "the big lady is *at least* yelling at me." If they're *capable* of the task and *resisting*, offer encouragement and then exit.

Do not be an audience. Being nearby is okay—just not an audience. Being an audience provides an opportunity for more drama and intensity. Don't give them that opportunity.

Firm *and* kind would be to offer one part you might be willing to do. So, if your child is getting dressed, for example—which can be a whole lot of clothes to put on if you're three—then let them know you're willing to do one part—like socks or pants—and they get to do the rest. That is firm *and* kind.

How to Hand Things Over, Options A to D

A - Ideal: As children age, we have to hand each task over to them gradually so as not to overwhelm them at eighteen when they leave us and haven't had practice mowing the lawn, feeding the dog, ordering for themselves, cooking, doing their own laundry, remembering for themselves, etc. We need to hand tasks over at each stage and age. As infants, when they're capable of putting themselves to sleep, we need to let them (painful as that may be). When they can feed themselves, we need to let them (messy as that may be). Remember, short-term pain yields long-term gain. They may be messy feeding themselves, but they'll get better at it with more practice. Them getting better at feeding themselves, dressing themselves, making their own bed or lunch, doing their own laundry, driving the car or mowing the grass means you are no longer doing this task for them. They own it and they feel capable. You can see their chest expand with the pride of ownership sometimes (after they get through their resistance). They feel good about themselves and see how capable they are of doing these tasks. We need to keep feeding them the opportunities at each age and stage. And, get out of their way. So, Option A is shutting our mouths and letting them take on the new task. Just know it will take them longer to complete a task than if you do it for them. They might not do it right, or the way you would. It might be messier than if you do it. But you've got to let all that go.

Short-term pain = long term gain.

B - Good: When you know you're still doing more for them than you should, remember to hand it over! And encourage them along the way.

C - Do no harm: Typically, C is doing nothing to intervene, and in this case, doing nothing is really harming them by continuing to enable/do tasks for them that we know they're capable of doing.

D - Harm: Belittling or shaming them as they try new tasks. Harming might also include nagging and reminding them, which robs them of an opportunity to learn and grow and build a new skill that they're capable of doing. We sometimes are not ready to hand it over. That is about us, not them. Harm also looks like us continuing to do these tasks for them. It can be enabling—enabling them to continue not to learn and to not be given the opportunity to grow at developmentally normal tasks.

Stay away from option D and you will be a perfEct parent.

TEN

The Evening Lament, Bedtime.
(And the morning rush!)

Talk about low resources. Bedtime.

This is the time of day when EVERYONE is tired. That's why we're headed to bed! It's a time that's ripe for power struggles: "Yes, you will" followed by "No, I won't."

"I need a drink of water!"

"Can we read another book?"

Or my personal favorite, "I'm not tired."

So, let's start at the beginning of the bedtime ritual.

This is the harrowing parenting ritual carried out every evening all across the world: getting our children to slow it down, turn it down, and then eventually turn off the machine that got them through the day. And from our kids' perspective, to do it when someone else is deciding for you *when* you need to do it?

How easy is it for YOU to do that?

Why would we expect it to be easier for them?

It can be easier, for sure. And, it helps to have that piece of data/ empathy with and for them during that time—it *is* hard to turn down all the stimulation the world provides to our senses, to still our bodies, still our minds, close our eyes, and fall into that very necessary and very restorative place: sleep.

First, I would like for you to recall a time when you were completely engrossed in something interesting: a project, a good book, a conversation. You were truly reveling in the experience. Now, imagine someone abruptly comes up to you and grabs the book and slams it closed, saying, "Time for bed!" Or, they do the same to interrupt your conversation or your project.

How are *you* feeling?

Safe to assume you're pretty annoyed, irritated and maybe even angry at the abruptness of this kind of interruption. Those emotions then get directed at the person who is causing us to terminate what we were enjoying so very much.

It's just plain rude.

That's what we do to our children nearly every night.

Going to bed is never as much fun as staying up. Our children feel like they're missing out on the goings-on. (You remember this feeling, don't you?) And, who wants to miss out? Not them.

How to impart that sense of empathy with and for them during this bedtime ritual? SAY IT! Let them know you understand how they feel.

"It's hard to go to bed when Mom and Dad are staying up."

"It's more fun to play LEGOs than it is to go to bed."

"Yes, you LOVE your book and it's hard to stop in the middle of a good story."

Remember step one of the three steps to setting a limit (Chapter 2)?

Understanding goes a long, long way.

It's far more important to any of us (big or little) that we are UNDERSTOOD than we get what we want.

That one is worth repeating: It is far more important to ANY of us that we are understood than we get what we want.

So, understand them. And acknowledge it.

It IS hard to go to bed.

And, let us not be rude.

> It is far more important to ANY of us that we are understood than we get what we want.

Let's begin the bedtime rituals with verbal warnings that a transition is coming—some version of "bedtime is in ten minutes" or set a timer that goes off in ten minutes so you're no longer the authority figure. The timer indicates bedtime. The timer is the bad guy, not you. You might not even need to say a word when it goes off. Simply head toward their bedroom. A wonderful invention for younger children who have yet to master the art of telling time is a device called Time Timer. It can be found online at timetimer.com. Wonderful invention. It has a red arch covering the time a child has allotted, and the red gets smaller and smaller as there is less and less time until finally there is no more red. Time is up. It quantifies time in a beautifully visual way. Any visual way for a young child to see that time is quantifiable helps. Older kids who know quantity (that three minutes is less than five minutes, for example) can use digital timers. These are brilliant investments.

How do we make bedtime more peaceful?

We set some limits.

Using the three steps to setting a limit (from Chapter 2) can be a beautiful practice at bedtime.

1. Empathize. Make them feel heard and understood.
    "Staying up is so much more fun than going to bed."

2. State the limit clearly, with no "but" at the beginning. Use a period or an "and."
    "It is eight o'clock, which is bedtime."

3. Give them a choice. What options do they have?
    "Would you like to wear these jammies or these jammies?
    Would you like Mom or Dad to read to you?
    Do you want to read two books or three books?
    Do you want to brush your teeth first or get your jammies on first?
    Would you like scrambled eggs for breakfast or oatmeal?
    Do you want to crawl upstairs or walk backwards upstairs?"

NOTE: Use only one set of the above choices. Don't barrage them with a bunch of decisions to make at the time of day when they're most depleted.

Some of your options are above. You can ALWAYS find a choice. It can be so very hard for us parents to find them sometimes. It's up to us to get outside of our box and come up with some different alternatives for them. We get stuck often in "it needs to be done like I said and when I said."

The truth is that you've always got a choice.

The choice isn't IF it's done.

The choice is HOW it's done.

And WHEN it is done.

With WHOM it's done.

WHERE it's done.

Not IF it's done.

We *are* going to bed. And, the who, where, when, how can all be made into options that provide a sense of power to your child. It's up to us to illuminate what those options are. They can also get stuck in tunnel vision: It needs to be done this ONE way and only this one way. In reality, there are many ways.

Let's help them see this.

An easy illustration of this: a little person with very little communication skills in a sandbox wants the green bucket. So, the only way they can think of getting it is to TAKE it forcefully from another child. Or, if they are really creative, they consider biting them. Tunnel vision. *There's only one way to get what I want.*

With some coaching and practice, they learn it might be more constructive to offer a trade of something to the green bucket holder OR verbally announce that he/she would like a turn with the bucket and wait OR ask to share it and take turns. All are options that can expand their tunnel vision when initially the child could only come up with one solution: bite. Under age four, children need assistance coming up with options. They need help getting out of their mental box. Over age four, they're more creative in their thinking and can come up with some options usually. They still need our help to get beyond the obvious choices though.

Back to that vexing time of day: bedtime. It's that time of day when your child is low on resources and you are, too. Both of the participants in the bedtime routine are just about depleted. Which is why we're all going to bed—to recharge our batteries in these bodies of ours. So, be kind and gentle to yourself about this and be kind and gentle to your children knowing this.

•••

CHARLIE WAS THREE YEARS OLD AND every night for many years our evening routine began the same way:

"Charlie, how many minutes do you need to be ready for bed?"

And we'd go back and forth until he'd negotiated a number between nine and twelve. (This gave *him* power in a daily situation he did not have power over). So, then he would meander himself up the stairs to begin the joyful adventures that lay ahead in his room and in the bathroom. There is so much to discover in those places at bedtime that was not available to discover during the day!

You know what I mean, right?

At least physically, he headed up there. He had a little printed guide on his bedroom wall that indicated what needed to be done: a picture of a toothbrush, a stick figure in jammies, and a book. He would do his thing (play, dawdle, occasionally be on task), and *one* of us would show up to his rocker at the agreed upon time. I would go into his room, sit in the rocker, and slowly begin the bedtime routine which, for us, began with reading.

Sometimes, he was ready.

Often, he was not.

That was not my problem.

Sometimes he was there and being read to, sometimes he was scurrying around trying to finish, and sometimes he was simply melting down on the floor in "the perfect fit." One time, I read the whole book to myself, rocked alone, and tucked no one into bed. I did all the parts alone. I went through the whole routine. I was available. He simply wasn't focused or ready. The real learning did not come that night.

It came on the following night in the form of "last night we didn't get to read the book together. I wonder what will happen tonight?" He learned these are logical consequences: tied to the event, making sense to him, not punitive or revengeful, and teaching him accountability. It's purely up to him whether he participates or not.

No yelling.

Lots of deep breathing on my part, however.

Short-term pain = long-term gain.

I was there, doing my part, providing the bedtime routine. The "perfect fit" might commence with, "Stop reading! I'm not ready! I haven't brushed my teeth yet!"

I would simply read softly and slowly. (If there was screaming, I would read silently.)

So, then HE would be rushing around, trying to finish. Occasionally, he missed the beginning of the book. The first few times, he would beg for me to restart. No go. These were natural consequences for the choices he made. After missing the first parts of the story a few times, his focus on his bedtime tasks got sharper. And, it helped him, as it helps most younger children, to have a printed visual key or guide they can reference with pictures of the bedtime tasks they need to complete. These can be pictures of them doing the task or cutouts from a magazine or drawings they make. They need to be involved in creating and posting them. Guides like these are also helpful to have for the morning routine and children can post them where they are easily referenced, such as a kitchen wall or door.

There was only one time I completed the entire bedtime routine to no one.

He never showed up.

Perhaps he was in his sister's room. I don't remember. What I *do* remember is the meltdown that occurred when he discovered I had already read the entire book, rocked a bit and lay in his bed with no one there.

That was a hard night for him.

Just because a child dawdles does not mean the parent is required to provide more time.

Firm and kind. That's how they learn.

This was funny sometimes with Charlie at age three with these bedtime negotiations. The number he agreed to was chosen by him (and had to work for me, hence the negotiation). And, it was simply a number he liked that night. He had no idea at the time that twelve minutes gave him more time than nine minutes. It wasn't about that. It was about *him* choosing the number and feeling powerful.

The key phrase in this Charlie-missed-an-entire-bedtime-routine story?

One time.

It only happened once. This is why what can look like a complete fiasco in the short term truly can be beautiful parenting in the long run. What is most important to consider is: what is the protocol I'm establishing for the NEXT time this situation occurs? (And there usually is a next time). A meltdown/"perfect fit" can be perfect parenting!

And what to do during the morning rush?

Ask questions rather than issue commands.

Ask questions rather than issue commands.

> Ask questions rather than issue commands.

Don't spoon feed your child what they need to do next or what they have yet to do. When we do this as parents, we're loaning them our brains/memory and they don't have to access or utilize ANY of their own brainpower, i.e., think for themselves. They simply allow whatever we say (and often repeat like a broken record over and over) to go in one ear and out the other, thinking all the while: *That big lady will tell me again. I don't have to remember.*

Why do they have that self-talk?

Because it's true.

We do.

We will give them the same information again and again. And they have the opportunity again and again to resist, ignore, forget.

No one wants to be told what to do or ordered around.

Not you.

Not them.

And, when you ask the open-ended question, "What do you still need to do to be ready?" their eyes will roll up toward the sky and they are THEN using their God given brains to THINK! They must actually use some mental power to come up with what they need to do next. This visual and mental activity is completely absent when we give them commands and spoon feed them.

> Ask, "what do you need to do to be ready?"

Remember: The questions that encourage your child to use their own brain the most are *open* ended: "What do you need to do to be ready?"

Second best questions? *Closed* ended… where YES or NO are the only available answers:

"Have you brushed your teeth? Are you ready for bed?"

The only possible response to "Have you brushed your teeth yet?" is yes or no.

The only possible response to "Are you ready for bed?" is yes or no.

Third in line: Spoon feeding them with commands.

This was always a clue for me in my own parenting.

If I'm sick of saying it, I can be certain they're sick of hearing it.

In those moments, I've become the broken record. And nobody wants to be *or* hear the broken record. That means I need to do something different.

This is not working.

And, as someone who teaches parenting strategies, the self-talk had an added layer to it for me.

Michelle, you TEACH this stuff! What can you do differently here? This is not working.

> If I'm sick of saying it, I can be certain
> they're sick of hearing it.

How to Handle Bedtime Struggles, Option A to D

A - Ideal: Empathize with your child. Verbally share with them your *true* understanding that going to bed is DEFINITELY not as fun as staying up. Offer the three steps to setting a limit: empathize, state the limit, offer choices. Ask questions rather than issue commands by not spoon feeding them their next steps. Agree to a timeframe with your child *before* they begin the bedtime routine and then do your part once the time has lapsed.

Offer open-ended questions: "What do you need to be ready?" Followed up usually with, "What *else* do you need to be ready?"

Offer choices so your child feels their need of power is being met at a time when they don't have power over bedtime occurring: "Do you want to wear the blue jammies or the red ones? This book or this book? Do you want to brush your teeth first or get your jammies on first?"

B - Good: Offer closed-ended questions where yes and no are the only possible responses.

"Have you done the teeth? Are the jammies on the body?"

C - Do no harm: "It's time to brush your teeth. It's time to get your jammies on." (And know that these are commands.).

Another version of "doing no harm" in regard to bedtime? Explain to your sweet kid that YOU don't have much in the tank tonight and that the bedtime routine needs to be shortened so you can get what you need. What a concept! Your child has the opportunity to hear that you have needs too and need some time, space, rest—or all three!

D - Harm: The usual bag of tricks here: yelling, shaming, spanking, pitting one child against the other in terms of speed, fostering competition (rather, have them try to beat their own time of getting ready). And, I offer this for your consideration: giving our children the answers over and over and over in the form of commands, reminders, telling them what they need to do IS harming them.

How?

It's robbing them of an opportunity to use their own brains and build their own muscle in regard to memory, organization, self-control, discipline. Whatever we do for them that they can do for themselves, we weaken in them. This weakening is from taking away an opportunity for them to build that muscle and grow.

I can't wait to be a grandparent. I don't have to groom *any* of this in them. I just get to enjoy…no firm, just kind. It will be my choice then as my grandchild has their own parent figures who are calling all the shots!

Stay away from option D and you are a perfEct parent.

A word on competition—it gets results.

And often, we promote it unknowingly.

It can sound as innocent as "Let's see who can get their jammies on faster" or "Who can be ready for bed first?" (Of course, this is if you have more than one child you're trying to corral at bedtime. Bless you.) Typically, thereafter follows a flurry of activity and they get the job done. So, what is wrong with that?

Pitting our kids against each other promotes the win/lose dynamic. One is going to emerge victorious and one is going to be disappointed. It can often turn even uglier after that if the victorious child chooses to gloat or brag at the expense of the slower child.

Why do we do this as parents? It gets results. It *looks* effective. They respond.

And, it comes at a price.

Instead, one idea, if they want to work against the clock, is to challenge them with their OWN time. For instance, "Last night, Grace, it took you eighty-six seconds to get your jammies on. I wonder how many seconds it will take you tonight?"

Or, "Last night it took you seven minutes and fifteen seconds to get ready for bed. How long do you think it will take you tonight?"

And, faster is not always better. Taking their time might be a beautiful thing. A leisurely pace might yield a peaceful entry to bed and sleep. That is what *we* are tasked to do for our bedtime routines—wind down, slow down, turn it down, relax.

There's so much competition out there in the world; it will never be eradicated. Yet, let's try to balance it out a bit in our homes.

You can offer a choice there as well. "If you take ten minutes or less to get ready for bed, we will have time to read two books.

If it takes you more time than ten minutes, we'll have time to read one book." This is said in a completely neutral tone that reveals no preference on your part. Hard to deliver in that way—and especially hard to deliver in a neutral tone when you *do* have a strong preference.

Regardless, it must be delivered that way if we are truly to meet the need for power in that moment for our child. If *our* preferences are stated or obvious, there's no real choice or power for our child. They're going to be reacting to us and often choosing the opposite of whatever our preference is so they too are exercising their power—even if that's not their preference.

Competition is everywhere for kids.

It's "I'm first. I'm swinging higher than her. I'm taller than him." One response that balances it out is to acknowledge the truth in their statement with a neutral tone of voice while acknowledging other truths. For instance, you could follow up "I got here first" with "Yes, you did. And she got here second and I got here third." All are true and factual. Watch the tone of voice here. Any inflection for first, higher, taller, etc., gives greater credibility to those.

Neutral tone.

Just the facts.

"I'm swinging higher than her" could be balanced with "Yes, and he is swinging lower than you." Or "I'm taller than him" yields "Yes, and he's shorter than you." This method gives no weight to one being more desirable over another.

Why bother? Because competition can breed quitters. If a competitor feels they can't win, then they may not even try. A child learns quickly what's more desired by the adults around him and becomes less willing to risk or try new things if he or she cannot excel at it.

That is a tragedy.

So many experiences in life are waiting for us to try, to dare greatly, and maybe to do them poorly—yet with courage, to do them at all. It is in the *doing* where the strength lies. Let's encourage our kids to be doers.

Stay away from option D and you will be a perfEct parent.

ELEVEN

Fighting

Whether it's minor pestering or out-and-out screaming matches, children's fighting can really get our emotions running hot and then we tend to react *immediately!* It drives us crazy! We soooo want our kids to like each other, be lifelong friends, negotiate, share, get along.

Those are *our* wants.

And, what do *they* want?

They just want the green bowl.

Well, not exactly.

They want more than the green bowl for their snack. They want us to *choose* them. They feel loved when we choose them over their sibling. And we're set up to FAIL in this win/lose dynamic.

Why?

Because someone *is* going to "lose" and not be given the green bowl, i.e., be chosen by us.

So, what are we to do with all this conflict?

Let's break it down.

Our job is to bring PEACE to the fight. There's already enough heat.

Emotions are high.

They're fighting for their space, their place, attention and ultimately love.

First, separate them to give them cool-off time. Do not, I repeat, DO NOT attempt to negotiate, rationalize, problem solve with children while they're in that heated state. If you wonder about the merit of this advice, consider how receptive *you* are to reason when you're unraveling. How much do *you* want to be talked to, lectured? When humans are angry, the limbic part of our brain has been activated and is LIT UP! It is wasted words and wasted energy to insert ourselves into that space.

So, you've given them time to separate.

Now, a word on "timeout."

It doesn't work.

In the traditional execution of it anyway.

Why is this?

Because the authority figure is in charge (has the power) over where the timeout occurs, how long it lasts, and—most importantly—the forced fact that it is happening at all.

They hate it.

They hate us.

Most children aren't sitting in timeout reflecting on their behaviors.

Rather, they're usually stewing about how they hate you, how stupid this is, any act of revenge they might exact to make them feel better. And, isn't this exactly *why* we're having them do it?

Because we want a change in their behavior?

We want them to recognize the error of their ways and modify it. Timeouts do not usually produce the outcome we want. Instead, it often turns into a power struggle about staying in the assigned location for the assigned timeframe—*that* is where the energy gets directed. Not usually where we *want* it to be directed, which is on the previous behavior that got them there in the first place.

What do we do?

So, let's start with separating them, if possible.

Even for a breath or two.

A beautiful fringe benefit of separation is that children begin to see interacting with a sibling or a friend IS A PRIVILEGE. We want to highlight this truth as parents by delivering that message over and over. Deliver it, yes, but not verbally, as that becomes nagging. Rather, by separating them when there is too much friction occurring. The children then begin to sense and receive the message, "I may need to manage *my* behavior differently if I want to play with my sibling…even if I want to be *around* my sibling."

> A beautiful fringe benefit of separation is that children begin to see interacting with a sibling or a friend IS A PRIVILEGE.

Accountability.

The message gets delivered over and over and over again by separating them when they demonstrate by their *own* choices that they can't be near each other.

Remember: I am 100 percent responsible for what I say and do.

My child is 100 percent responsible for what they say and do.

NO MATTER WHAT IS SAID OR DONE TO ME.

When I truly believe this, I have to live in the consequences of my own choices and not blame someone else for my own choice.

Blame.

It's so much easier to offload our accountability and blame to someone else.

Blame our sibling.

Blame our parents.

Blame the weather.

Blame our spouse.

Blame our child.

In the words of my sister growing up, "My arm did it."

The truth is: **We are 100 percent responsible for what we say and do, no matter what is said or done to us.**

This is not a message we hear very much in our culture.

More often, we hear this message: If you yell at me, I can yell back at you. If you hit me, I can hit you back. If you treat me unkindly, I am justified in exacting revenge on you and hurting you back.

> We are 100 percent responsible for what we say and do, no matter what is said or done to us.

If you yell at me, you're responsible for that.

If I choose to yell back at you, I'm responsible for that.

If you hit me, you're responsible for that.

If I hit you back, I'm responsible for that.

We are 100 percent responsible for what we say and do no matter what is said or done to us. We are 100 percent responsible for managing our own behaviors and emotions—that's what it boils down to.

It is helpful to deliver this message to children in an experiential way.

The self-talk inside the child becomes: "I'm going to be removed from this activity if I don't do something different here." And, that may mean that if their sibling is bothering them, that *they* move themselves away or to another room before *they* do something that gets them in trouble. (Hitting, yelling, biting, destruction of property, and on and on).

Accountability.

Accountability is the result after many opportunities of practicing this.

So, if possible, separate the children. Separation can occur in any space or room. It's not limited to their bedroom.

One of my children would find their bedroom to be an acceptable calming area whereas with my other child, sending her to her room would only escalate the emotion. She preferred to be near the family on the couch.

If we want to meet our child's need of power, it can be helpful to have them designate a space for themselves ahead of time that they'd like to calm in *before* that moment arises again and again. You may even want to encourage them to place calming objects in that space for themselves to welcome them there when the time arises. An auditory child might like music to calm themselves, a kinesthetic child might prefer to go shoot hoops or run around outside to calm themselves. Some might like to scribble or rip paper or pound something. The idea is to provide an outlet, a space for this. It's a place and space to "rinse" out their emotions.

Next, *when they're ready*, they come out of this space (which *could* even be the playroom) when *they* feel calm. When *they* have the mental space to discuss.

That may take them one minute or all morning.

It's up to them.

Here are a few helpful questions to ask that can trigger the accountability referenced earlier.

For younger children, these can be verbally asked, and for older kids, you might want to write these down so they can have them in or near their space for a visual queue of what self-reflection is needed:

- What is the problem?
- What is MY part of the problem?
- What is one thing I could do differently next time?

When *they* are able to answer those questions for themselves, that indicates they're finished calming and reflecting. If they're not ready to answer those, then they just earned themselves more time.

As I have heard some teachers phrase it, they've earned "the gift of time."

This time for themselves is to re-center, regroup, refocus, and calm.

It's best when modeled by the parents.

DO THIS YOURSELF.

"Who you are speaks so loudly I can't hear anything you're saying."

Remember? They're not listening to our words. Rather, they're watching us. We are their first teachers.

If we parents hit our child, we are teaching them to hit their siblings or friends.

If we parents yell at our child, we are teaching them to yell as a way to communicate.

If we parents model patience when frustrated, we are teaching them to be patient with themselves.

If we parents speak kindly to our partners, we are showing them how to speak kindly to their siblings and friends.

> Who you are speaks so loudly I can't hear anything you're saying.

If we parents show respect for ourselves and our bodies, we're teaching them to respect themselves and their bodies.

It's that simple.

Telling a child to "Do as I say, not as I do" is not effective.

They're watching EXACTLY that. They're watching what we DO.

Also, if the fight is about an object, as the parent you must remove the object at the outset.

What do I mean by this?

If they're fighting over a toy, take away the toy.

Completely remove it from their grasp, from the room. No one gets the toy.

It does not matter who owns it or who had it first.

It is now in No Man's Land.

I used to put the object on a ledge in our kitchen.

Very visible.

Out of circulation does not mean it's out of mind.

They need to see they haven't yet "worked it out" about that object.

And, they also need to see it's not about that object.

Which is why the heat around that object dissipates when they realize you're going to "put them in the same boat" [by removing the object] and make them BOTH responsible for the fight.

"What do you mean, Mom? He took it from me! I had it first!"

Putting them in the same boat means it doesn't matter who started it or who had it first.

It.

Does.

Not.

Matter.

How can I say that? You may be wondering.

Well, we want to make the kids responsible for their own conflict. They're responsible for working it out. They're responsible for *caring* that their sibling wants a turn with their item.

This does NOT mean surrendering their needs to the other sibling. This does not mean abandoning themselves (complete with the future resentment that surely will ensue). What it means is they have to care about the other person. Each has to listen. The feelings of both are equally important. And, they have to be invested in seeing if there's a solution that would work for *both* parties. It does not need to be equitable. It just needs to work for both parties.

Let's get deeper into this heated topic.

Our intervention:

First, remove the object.

Second, separate the children.

Then, once they've had time to re-center, now it's time to bring them back together to work through the conflict.

Be warned that at this point, their motivation to do so may be very low. Especially since they've received the message that you're not going to intervene, be a private investigator, referee, or choose sides.

That's what they're seeking.

They want you to choose them.

Over their sibling.

Why?

It sends them the message that they're loved.

While sending our children messages that they're loved is healthy, this is not the time—during a conflict—to send it. It comes at the expense of someone else, their sibling.

So, often the fights are attempts for you to "choose them." When they're NOT chosen, this prompts the other child to need to initiate a fight, i.e., another opportunity down the road where THEY'RE chosen or acknowledged and feel the love as well. It can become an unconscious future goal—to get their sibling in trouble so they can feel loved too.

You can easily observe this when one child is misbehaving and then the other child wants you to notice *they're* doing the right thing. Then, *they* feel loved by you.

You know what I mean, right? When one sibling is completely off the rails and the other child wants to be acknowledged for what they're doing correctly?

It's a bid for love.

Unfortunately, it comes at the expense of the other child's pain.

Let's become aware of this and stop encouraging this dynamic. It promotes the ego's need to be superior to someone else so we can feel better about ourselves. The other must be deemed inferior.

Instead, a compassionate response would acknowledge we ALL have these moments of "being off the rails" and we can give space, time, patience to their sibling to come back to themselves.

The heart wins instead of the ego winning with that kind of response.

Our job, in regard to fighting, is to help them resolve their conflicts.

Not choose sides.

Not problem-solve for them.

I didn't know this either.

I believed if I did a REALLY good job being a private investigator, I would get to the truth of what was going on and then render a solution that would be well-received given the thoroughness of my investigation.

Are you with me here?

Are you familiar with this?

Well, does it *ever* work for you?

It didn't for me.

My thoroughness was not well-received. That was a fantasy land.

So, how to deal?

First, when, or if, they're motivated to revisit the issue—which oftentimes they are not—ask **each child what they want.** Common responses include: "I want the toy. I want to build my plan without him knocking it down. I want the blue bowl."

We've all heard these. The list goes on and on.

Second, after each child states what they want, **have the other child *repeat back*** to them what they said. This results in a clear understanding of what is wanted by both children. That may resolve some things right there up front. What is *really* wanted. Maybe they're just wanting some attention and the way they're going about it is not getting them what they want? Maybe they really want to play with the other child and knocking down the blocks was their crude (and ineffective) delivery method regarding that want. Maybe they want to see the new birthday toy of their sibling and they want to get them in trouble so they can get a turn with that? Maybe they're simply feeling out of sorts and want to share their misery and pick a fight? Maybe they're bored? (I remember that feeling as a kid…picking a fight based on boredom…it gets the energy flowing for sure!)

Then, after EACH child has stated what they want and the other child has REPEATED what the other wants, then **brainstorm** ideas to solve the situation.

Make sure to set the ground rules for brainstorming before you begin: All ideas are fair game. Do NOT evaluate any idea as "good" or "bad." Rather, use the line: "That's an idea!" or "There's another idea!" It can be hard for us to deliver impartiality at the beginning of this practice. But it's important to create a safe atmosphere for all ideas to be heard.

The reason for allowing all ideas? Because even the "bad" ones? (e.g., "I could kick him and take the toy") have already been thought of. So, they are valid. We must allow our child to express them. Even the "bad" ideas qualify as ONE of their possible solutions.

"I could bite him." That's one idea.

"I could hit him with the stick." Yes, that's another idea.

"I could have the toy all day." There's an idea.

"I always get the iPad." Yes, that's one idea.

Stay with me here.

So, make sure **there are *at least* three ideas**. If they're under age four, you can help them generate ideas. They have tunnel vision and biting or hitting may be all they've got in terms of problem solving. Over age four, they can come up with some more creative options on their own. Remember, all ideas get listed.

Once the brainstorming is complete, **restate the list of ideas** to your kids. Now instruct them to choose which idea they're going to implement. Tell them to talk amongst themselves and decide which one idea they want to do. Let them know they *both* need to agree, and to let you know when they've come to an agreement.

This is why all ideas get listed.

Your kids are likely NOT going to agree to one of them having the toy all day or one of them ALWAYS having the iPad or picking the movie for the family, or hitting their sibling, etc.

And then?

Get out of their way. Once they present their plan, let it happen.

As far as their negotiations go, it doesn't matter what does or doesn't work for you, the parent.

It's not about you.

It only has to work for them.

So, when they agree the younger child gets to have the iPad for twelve minutes and the older child gets to have it for fifteen minutes, it's our job NOT to intervene with any kind of lecture or admonishment about the younger child getting less time. (Unless this happens as a pattern every time—at which point it's okay to tell them the solution doesn't work for you). Otherwise, stay out of it.

It only has to work for them.

Their negotiations will get more sophisticated with time and practice.

If they're choosing to alternate time with an item, it's helpful to get some details about the transition of said item or the timeframe. For instance, you'll want to know if they each get the item for five minutes and then switch. Or one gets it till lunch and the other gets it after lunch until dinner. Or one has it today and the other has it tomorrow. The key is to take yourself out of being the authority here. Encourage them to set a timer and when the timer goes off the other child is free to use the item.

The timer then becomes the authority.

We have that position of authority naturally every day. Our children are fatigued of listening to us. It's quite astonishing to see how effective timers become when they're the authority and no words come out of our mouths. The fact is, children can become "parent deaf" and hear everything except us. It's like the Charlie

Brown mom. They just hear noise, and nothing sinks in.

Use the timer.

Now, a word on the child who consistently "gives in" or compromises in the agreement stage, allowing the other one to get their preference met…

This is the *one* case when you need to intervene in their problem-solving. Only if this is a pattern. When this continually happens, you should say something like: "That doesn't work for me." (Even though none of the other times worked for you either. Remember, it's not about you.) Say this only when there's a *pattern* of one child abdicating their wants repeatedly.

So, if the fight is over an object? One solution is they agree to a timeframe where each can enjoy that object separately. When it's the abdicator's time for it, you can say that it's perfectly fine if they don't want to play with/use it right now. If that's the case and they don't want to use it, then it's off limits during that time for the other child. It sits stagnate.

This message is huge for the child giving up his or her needs.

They *matter* as well.

They are each important.

•••

CHARLIE AND GRACE WERE FOUR AND SIX years old when I overheard this conversation taking place in the playroom:

"We better work it out or she is going to take it!"

I smiled.

That felt so good.

After many, many conversations facilitating this process between them, they were getting it. They knew no one would win if the other didn't also win.

They *had* to care about the other to get what they wanted.

And what a beautiful message that is in our world.

I have to care about you to get what I want.

It warmed my heart then and still does.

How to Handle Fighting Between Kids, Option A To D

A - Ideal: Take the time to teach the steps for resolving conflict with these kids. Over and over and over again. It will take many times. It's not about the green bowl; remember that. Put them in the same boat. Make them both responsible for the fight. Nobody gets the movie, iPad, green bowl, until we come up with a solution that works for *both* of you. This works whether it's your own kids or your child and a friend.

Remember: the solution does not need to work for you, the parent.

Give time for cooling off.

Have them come back together and answer the three questions:
- What is the problem?
- What is my part in the problem?
- What's one thing I could do differently next time?

Or, after they're calm, facilitate them resolving the conflict.

1. Ask each child to state what they want.
2. Have each child repeat what the other wants.
3. Open the floor to brainstorm solutions. Leave in all the "bad" ideas. All ideas get listed.
4. Allow the two children to choose the solution that works for them.

All the while, you're putting them in the same boat. They each have to CARE about the other. In time, they'll learn that nobody wins if I don't consider what my sibling/friend wants.

Wouldn't countries benefit from this type of conflict resolution? Let's teach it over and over and over again.

B - Good: Give both children the "thinking chair" instead of timeout. If time is limited, simply separating them without the problem solving added is okay. Or, the conflict resolution process can be moved to a later time.

C - Do no harm: If children bickering is bothering you and there's no physical harm occurring (i.e., you're just annoyed), then YOU take a timeout. Move yourself out of the room. Go outside. Take a walk. Listen to music. Count. Breathe.

Do no harm.

We're often annoyed listening to the negotiations. They can drag on and on. Manage your own annoyance yourself *if* your children are being patient with each other, not getting physical, not yelling, and continuing to work things out.

•••

THE KIDS AND I WERE STANDING AROUND a bonfire at my dad's. They were seven and nine years old. They began arguing about a "fire stick." They were negotiating whose turn it was, who had laid it down, who had found it first, etc. This was dragging on and on. My dad and I were nearby also engaged in a conversation. He was annoyed listening to them and believed he was helping, so he said, "You two stop fighting." I said, "Dad, they're working it out. If it's annoying, then we should move." They were not yelling at each other. They weren't waving a fire stick at each other. They weren't getting physical with each other. They were *negotiating*. Sometimes it can go on longer than any of us wants to listen. And, is that not what we're trying to get them to do? Listen to each other and find a solution that works for both of them without getting physical?

If *we* get annoyed, then *we* need to leave the room. Do Option C. They clearly are doing just fine. In fact, they are doing better than fine. They're resolving their conflict. Well.

D - Harm: Engaging in the fight and modeling the very same behavior that's frustrating you is Option D here: physically harming the child, overpowering the child, shaming, yelling, isolating them.

Remember: I'm 100 percent responsible for what I say and what I do.

Model that.

Stay away from option D and you will be a perfEct parent.

TWELVE

How Do I Get My Child to Do Their Homework? Without a World War?

The short answer is:

Give them power to manage the homework and after-school schedule.

When will it get done?

Where will it be done?

What subject do they want to start with first?

Not, *if* it's done.

It's all about empowering them with choices, remember? Have a conversation (ideally out of the moment, e.g., when driving or during a shared activity like a game or cards or basketball or cooking) about the various tasks they need to complete after coming home from school. You can mention topics like shower, snack, play/relax, homework, dinner, etc.

Then, ask your child in what order those work best for him or her? Where in the house would they like to do their homework? And when—before or after playing/relaxing? Right after school or later in the evening? And, as the parent, you're always invited to share what works for you, or what doesn't work for you, in regards to their proposed plan.

Before sharing too many of your opinions, let them try out *their* homework schedule for an agreed upon period of time. Maybe one week? Then commit to revisiting the plan with them where you both share your observations about how that week went. Based on that talk, then modify the plan for the upcoming week with those learnings. Write out and post the homework schedule somewhere as a reference tool.

Remember, parent: This is *their* plan. Let them live in the consequences of *their* plan.

Keep in mind that grades don't matter until high school.

Okay, so I have been corrected a few times—that grades *may* really matter in seventh or eighth grade if the child is *applying* to a particular high school. In that case, grades do not matter until seventh grade! So, we can relax a bit around this grade situation. The early years are the ones where we can help build good habits and allow our child to be held accountable and responsible for their *own* homework.

A NOTE:

Parents, be careful about using the "we" language. You have already been to third grade. So, "WE" do not have a lot of homework tonight. Your CHILD, however, may have a lot of homework tonight. There's a collective identity that sometimes needs to be separated when parents refer to themselves as active in the *child's* event.

"WE have practice tonight." No, you are not on the soccer team.

"WE have a big project due on Friday." WE do not. They do.

If you're enjoying their projects or sports too much, you may need to find other creative outlets for yourself. It's THEIR school and THEIR project and THEIR practice. You've already had the experience of school—all it was for you and maybe all that it wasn't. It is your child's turn now. Mentally separate yourself from your child if you find yourself using that "we" language. And, find outlets for yourself. If this is you—what a relief, you no longer have homework to do!

Now, about that homework. The first semester of first grade, stay involved. Help the kids get organized. Teach them how this school thing works. Teach them good organizational habits. Asking, "Where do you need your folder to be to remember it in the morning? Where do you need your backpack to be? Do you want to lay out your clothes tonight or pick them out in the morning?"

Remember, this is all new for them. First grade. Desks. Maybe they're even changing classes. All big stuff after kindergarten.

Then, about midway through first grade, work on backing yourself out of involvement. I let each of my kids know I would no longer be willing to remind them about things they needed to remember. It's the difference between help and support. Help is doing something FOR someone that they may or may not be able to do for themselves. And help is often needed at times. Support is coaching or aiding someone with the goal that they'll then be able to do it for themselves eventually. My exit midway through first grade was with an eye toward *supporting* each of them. And, letting them fail and feel that moment of "Ugh, I forgot that at home!"

If we save them from that moment, they will not learn. It has been painful to watch the faces over the years of parents as I tell them I don't want them to drive homework, backpacks or lunches to school to their child when they forget them at home.

The parents become a bit panicked. Some turn white. Some turn on me. It's entertaining to watch.

We are hardwired instinctually to protect our children. Mama

Bear and Papa Bear are in us. And, it's *necessary* to override that instinct at times. If our children are going to experience hurt, feel disappointment, and feel failure—and they all will—then we want that to happen while they're in our homes and have our support through it. They can then know they're loved and cared for even WHEN they fail, hurt or disappoint themselves or us.

> If our children are going to experience hurt, feel disappointment, and feel failure—and they all will—then we want that to happen while they're in our homes and have our support through it.

Children often mistakenly believe they're loved *conditionally*— that we, as parents, will only love them if they do what we want. They need to be shown and told over and over and over again, "I love you AND it's not okay to hit your brother. I don't care for the whining, AND I love you." We're separating the deed from the doer. "I love you even when you forget your backpack. Yes, you failed your test today and it seems you're really discouraged about that. What would you like to do about it? How can I help?" And, "I love you no matter what grades you get."

Remember these are *their* grades and their experiences. Keep the focus on that. Empower them with your questions. What grades do *they* want to get this semester? How can they get there? What specific ideas do they have to improve their science grade? Is there any way to help them? A great question is simply to ask, "How can I help?"

It is not about what WE want or expect from them.

Food, eating, potty training, and grades.

These all can become HUGE power struggles between parents and children. And, ultimately, the power rests squarely on the child's shoulders for each of these. We cannot make them swallow food. We cannot force them to eliminate waste from their bodies. And, we cannot do school for them. (Well, some parents try. And, teachers know exactly whose project was done by the child and whose were done by the parents).

To aid our children in getting their homework done, we need to do the opposite of what we're likely doing now. We need to get out of the way. Let THEM own their plan, own their homework, own their results. And, stay involved by caring. By being available. Asking questions (preferably open ended rather than closed ended) about how their plan is working for them and how it may need to be changed.

•••

GRACE OWNED HER HOMEWORK PLAN UNTIL she didn't. She forgot to do her homework. And it bothered her. I watched and let it happen. And then it happened again two weeks later.

When something occurs sporadically, exceptions can be made. Exceptions *should* be made. I HAVE taken a backpack to school before. I have taken a needed paper to school before. And, those items were delivered to my kids when they *typically* did not forget things. There was no pattern. "Every once in a while" does not constitute a pattern for me. However, one time one week and then another time the next week does constitute a pattern.

The second time, the answer is no.

So, Grace again forgot to do her homework two weeks after the first missed assignment. It was then that I stepped in and let her know her after-school schedule was going to be decided by me for *one week*. And, the order of my plan was: snack, relaxation, and then homework prior to dinner. She was required to do my plan for one week. (She was ten at the time.) The following week she was free to go back to her after-school homework plan and try again.

Natural and logical consequences. They are the most effective learning tools.

How to Get your Child to Do their Homework, Option A to D

A - Ideal: Dialogue about a schedule after school. Ask, what is the order of things that works best for them? Where? Before or after snacking/showering/playing? And then get out of their way and let them execute their plan for an agreed upon period of time and see how it goes.

B - Good: Ask closed-ended questions about homework. Have you done your homework? Have you finished your math?

C - Do no harm: If there are big power struggles going on in your home currently surrounding homework, the "do no harm" plan would be to stop talking about it. Give yourself three or four days and see what happens. Manage your own frustration/feelings about it. Let them own their problem.

Remember, you already graduated from third grade.

D - Harm: Shaming, bribing, yelling, threatening, doing it for them, creating a dependency on you for their homework routine by doing it all with you by their side or micromanaging their work.

Stay away from option D and you will be a perfEct parent.

THIRTEEN

What's the Difference Between Encouragement and Praise?

Did you know there's a difference?
I didn't.

Praise is easier to see and is much more common. It is outside of us. It is someone ELSE's opinion of us. If we truly break it down, it's a form of judgment. And, praise focuses on the outcome/end result. It's often superlative and generalized. It is conditional upon an event/performance. It is external.

Examples of praise are endless, and they FLY out of our mouths without us really being conscious of the subtle impact they may be having:

You're such a good girl.

You are the best painter.

Your drawings are beautiful!

You're such a good (insert sport) player.

You're such a good helper.

The subtle impact? The words SOUND positive. And they can also ring hollow to the receiver. How? Why?

Well, as the child, if I'm receiving over and over the message that I'm such a good girl when I DO something you approve of, it seems the love you have for me only exists when I *do* those things. And, I'm not even sure WHAT those things are as it's often generalized and vague.

You know how your kids bring you picture after picture that they painted or drew? I received a WHOLE lot of rainbow and flower pictures. I got so many they all seemed to blend together. If I consistently deliver the same version of the same message to my daughter, "What a great painting!" or "You're such a great artist!" the message SOUNDS positive. Heard over and over again, praise can become vacuous.

Words without feeling.

We can really distinguish the difference between encouragement and praise when we can experience how different encouragement feels *after* experiencing how praise feels.

Unlike praise, encouragement is internal. It's how we feel about ourselves and our own performance. It's not focused on the end result/outcome; rather the focus is on the process or the journey and the *effort* involved. Encouragement is *specific* in its wording. It's detailed and not global or general. It's not superlative. It sees the other as a human who is putting forth an effort toward something and not a performance or product.

Shifting our verbiage from praising statements to encouraging statements can sometimes feel like a foreign language. It can be awkward, and I've heard it described as "flat."

Examples include:

"You worked really hard on that painting. You've been over at that table for forty-five minutes. Tell me about your painting."

Then, actually listen.

And if you would like to share after they've talked about their painting and how they created it, make your comments specific. "I see you used glitter on your rainbow this time. Or, I see that you used purple in these flowers. I haven't seen you use that before."

Notice, these comments are not judgments.

Rather, they are observations.

"I noticed in the game you got three rebounds. How do you feel *you* played today?"

"How do you feel about your grades?"

"What do *you* want them to be?"

"How did you improve science from a B- to a B+?"

"How can I help you reach your goals?"

Here's a sideline huddle for parents: bring it in. There's one universal question that seems to fly out of our mouths after our children's athletic events. Do you know what it is?

It is this: "Did you win?"

That question is a praise-focused question. It's focused on outcome alone. Your child may very well have had the best performance *they* have ever had, AND the team may have lost. That can feel rather discouraging and confusing to a child.

An encouraging alternative?

"How did you play?"

Then LISTEN to the answer. Be specific in your observations, not global or generalizing.

"I noticed you really did pass more today. Was that something you were focusing on?"

"What are you most proud of?"

And, certainly you can share some part you enjoyed watching. "I love watching you play."

"I noticed how you dribbled around number twenty-five, and

then passed it to John and he scored." Observations like that are detailed and specific.

Those are the ones that feel most real. They're the ones that make it into our hearts. They feel genuine.

The important point here is to keep the focus on your child and *their* experience of the event—not oversimplifying the experience down to winning or losing. When we do that, the message we're delivering to our child is that winning is what is important to you. And, your child may have very little power/influence over that. What they DO have power and influence over is their own individual contribution/performance. And that IS something they can break down/talk about/set goals for/improve.

We, as parents, are never going to eradicate praise. It's everywhere in our culture. What we *can* do, however, is balance it in our homes with a *whole* lot of encouragement instead of praise.

We're raising praise junkies—kids who are looking outside of themselves for external validation and approval. This may be a harsh visual, but it helps drive it home for me.

They're becoming addicts to praise. We have become addicts to praise.

Imagine our children are being conditioned with so much praise that they're holding out their arm as if drug addicted, asking: *Who is going to give me my next hit? SOMEBODY outside myself needs to tell me how great I am.* And then I need more and more and more of that. So, who is going to tell me? Who is going to "like" my posts on social media? Who is going to tell me I'm okay? Who out there can do that for me?

Instead, I ENCOURAGE you to ENCOURAGE your children.

Notice their efforts. Acknowledge how much time they practiced. How much effort they put into their homework or their painting or their poem or their bed making or learning to ride their bike. Verbally share how you saw they had three seconds of air where they were going on that bike with no assistance. When we see/feel/experience that we CAN do something, we're likely to grow that skill or talent. It's a capable place. And, it feels good.

And, it brings your child back to how they feel about *themselves*. Not how you, the parent, feel about them. They're able to tune in. Tune *inside* instead of *outside* for validation.

ENCOURAGE your children.

It's not that we can't ever praise our children. You certainly can. When you choose to praise your kid with the superlative terms: BEST, MOST WONDERFUL, GREATEST, etc., give those words when they're *not* conditioned upon any performance of theirs.

They just are.

Here are some examples:

You're the BEST kid I could ever have. (Not because they just made their bed)

You're the greatest boy EVER! (Not because he pooped on the potty)

You're the most wonderful young lady! (Not because she was nice to her sister)

Just say those things.

Out of the blue.

Simply because you feel them.

And, mostly? Because they need to hear them.

•••

GRACE LOVED TO DRAW AND PAINT when she was little. There was a stage in her life where flowers, and scenes with flowers and rainbows, were the picture of the day. Sometimes, more than one a day. Many of the paintings looked like duplicates of the previous ones. I was SO glad I had learned the difference between praise and encouragement when she was one. Otherwise, I would have been stuck saying the same thing with each painting! Instead, I tried hard to focus on the subtle. What made this painting unique? What mediums did she choose to use in it? Where did she want to hang the painting now that she was finished with it? For it to be believable, I had to be specific for each painting. I observed her joy in creating it. Then she moved into a photography stage where she would take these spectacular photographs of flowers around the neighborhood.

Here are some *encouraging* words that came of out my mouth:

"You love to paint."

"Thank you for showing me."

"This painting has both paint and crayon on it. That's creative!"

"Ooooooo look at the color/petal/stem/leaves of that flower!"

"You have an eye for capturing a photo. I like how this one is zoomed in on the flower."

"Tell me about your painting." (That is my favorite line as it gives your child full authority to speak of their work).

How to Focus on Encouragement Over Praise, Option A to D

A - Ideal: Say *encouraging* words to your children—these are specific, based on observations, and focus on the effort involved (as opposed to *praise* words, which include loads of superlatives, focused on outcomes, and are judgments of your child and their performance)

B - Good: Catch yourself on the numerous times you want to praise and bite your lip. And, then awkwardly construct something out of your mouth that is not praise, but encouragement. It WILL be awkward for while! It certainly was for me when I learned this.

C - Do no harm: Rest "on the sidelines" and leave out praise AND encouragement until you can find something encouraging to say.

D - Harm: Constantly praising them with hollow compliments, creating a praise junkie who looks outside of themselves for approval because we, the parents, have unconsciously/ inadvertently trained them to do so. Because of our empty platitudes, they've become hooked on other people recognizing and affirming them instead of building their own internal muscle of capacity and self-evaluation.

Stay away from option D and you will be a perfEct parent.

FOURTEEN

How Do I Get Her to Clean Up the Playroom? Or Her Bedroom?

The dreaded task: cleanup.

Does ANYONE really enjoy cleaning up from ANYTHING?

The answer often is, *sometimes.*

Same for our kids. Cleaning up is NEVER as much fun as creating—creating the mess, creating the plan, creating the art, creating the project, etc.

Cleaning up is simply not that exciting.

So, that's the first piece for us to understand as we try to coerce our little darlings into tidying up! It's understandable they resist this task. *We* resist this task in preference to other enjoyable things.

And, it must be done.

Our homes don't clean themselves. Usually, someone needs to feel accountable for the task and feel ownership for the job to get done. Often, there is visual chaos that makes it feel like our house is closing in on us! Our eyes relax with less to see. Less stimulation. More Zen. Peace.

A playroom is definitely NOT Zen. So what are we to do instead of remind, coax, bribe, lecture?

Those moments when I found myself being the broken record with the same thing coming out of my mouth over and over (lecturing)—*that* was a reminder to me that I needed to consider how to do it differently. The playroom was one of those a-ha moments.

I didn't need it to be cleaned daily. (You might). For me, it was about day three when I started to snap and realize I was nowhere near my Zen place.

One way to counteract the urge to lecture in this situation is to substitute words or signals. Teachers are masters at this. For instance, a flick of the lights may indicate it's time for the kids to line up. That visual queue conditions them to prepare to do something…like get in line. For me, many years ago, in Teach for America, my kindergarten children would signal that they needed to go the bathroom by putting their hand up with their peace fingers crossed. No words. A nod or a look from me indicated they were free to leave the room to take care of themselves. All wordless!

Signals work.

In some preschools, children are taught to sing a cleanup song. So, you could have one of those in your home. OR, you could choose your own fun dance cleanup song. Do you realize how fun it is to clean while you're dancing? Or maybe even compile a clean-up playlist of a few dance songs! Kids are masters at play. It's their language. So speak it. Speak the play language and make it as fun as you possibly can.

···

So back to my "day three from my Zen place" story when the playroom was closing in on me? I used a small wooden train whistle that was a birthday party favor. We all agreed that if they heard the whistle, that meant they were needed in the playroom and they had ten minutes to do the best cleaning job they could in there. It didn't need to be perfect—the playroom cleanse/overhaul is not what I'm talking about here. Rather, just an everyday, "good enough" cleanup task. I would then set the timer on the microwave for ten minutes.

It worked.

And it worked SO much better than my lecture. It was really quite magical. I'd blow this little thing and they would actually stop what they were doing and toddle, sometimes RUN, into the playroom to do their thing for ten minutes. It felt relieving for me and sometimes even exciting for them. They just did it! It was like that little wooden whistle had superpowers. Maybe it did?

Or maybe it was just that I was no longer the authority figure harping at them.

I set an expectation.

It was delivered as stated.

And they honored it.

The timer would go off after ten minutes and they would stop cleaning or simply play with whatever treasure had been uncovered in those ten minutes! Magic.

Expectation setting is important. What does *your* everyday, "good enough" cleanup look like? You need to share that with them when y'all discuss the signal, word, or song that will indicate it's time to clean the playroom. Does the carpet all need to be cleared? Books on shelves? Costumes in trunk? Legos in bins?

Be clear.

As a psychotherapist, I have had the sincere privilege of listening to the challenges that occur inside many homes. Sometimes expectations and lack of communication around them are part of the issue. For instance, I have heard that one partner would like more "help" around the house from the other. And, the other party has defended that they DO help. In fact, they just did the dishes last night.

Maybe "help" by one's definition is not the occasional dish washing, but instead, owning that task every day.

Maybe one's definition of help is going to the grocery this week? Maybe it's going to the grocery EVERY week?

Define what kind of "help" you need.

Be clear.

Be specific.

So, be clear in your house with what your expectations are. What "help" really is. And, this certainly applies to the playroom. Be clear on what "clean" means to you. If you need it to be a ten on a scale of one to ten, be clear about that. If you need it to be a five or six, be clear about that. It's your call.

...

SPEAKING OF HELP, I ALWAYS BELIEVED I would have four children. I wanted to have four. I biologically birthed two. However, my dream came true in my two nieces, Eberle and Cecilia.

I adore them.

And, our four children grew up like siblings. Those two girls know what it's like to have a brother because of Charlie—for better or for worse!

And, on the subject of helping, in my house if you asked any of our four children privately this very same question, you would most certainly receive the very same answer. The question is this: "What is *THE* question?" (Yes, that really is the question).

Each of them would answer exactly the same.

They would answer: "How can I help?"

Around my house, if it's not obvious visually or intuitively how to help in a situation or help a person, these four kids have each been instructed (over and over and over again) to ask THE question. "How can I help?" Doesn't it feel good to be asked that?

A word on pacing.

Regarding cleaning, be that the playroom, their bedrooms, or anything else you have convinced them to clean, keep pace with THEIR pace. What I mean by that is this: if they're going slow, then you go slow. If they're expeditious, then you be expeditious. Them dawdling does not mean I will be working harder and doing their job.

And, I often stated that out loud as an observation: "It looks like you're going slow today. Okay, I'll go slow. too." Or, "it looks like you're really speedy this afternoon, I'll also be speedy."

Them dawdling doesn't mean you will pick up the slack. Don't get ahead of them.

Also, it's realistic to expect a child of age eight or older to be able to clean and organize with some independence. Prior to age eight, it's much more productive if you participate in a parallel type way, working alongside them. A child younger than eight tasked with cleaning their room or the playroom most often finds it to be a treasure trove of fun discoveries! It's not really a focused task. Their attention span is too short. They have so very much to *discover* in the room or playroom!

How to Get Your Kids to Clean, Option A to D

A: - Ideal: When you're OUT of the moment, discuss a word or signal or song or playlist that means it's time to clean the playroom. Also determine how much time will be devoted to this task.

IN the moment, set a timer. Or let the songs play. Everyone cleans!

When the timer ends, time is up.

Keep pace with their pace of cleaning.

One mom who has my respect (she has five children, two sets of twins) used a certain song as her signal in the morning that indicated: when this song ends, it's time to be in the car ready to go to school. She said her mornings became so very peaceful. I imagined the six of them being like the Pied Piper…she heads out to the car and they peacefully follow.

B - Good: Use the signals you've agreed upon and the children do the job without you participating. It might be helpful to lower your expectations at this point. Maybe you'll be getting a four or five (out of 10) out of the job? Or lower them even further, that ANYTHING they do is better than it was previously?!

C - Do no harm: Leave the playroom messy as it is and wait until you can communicate the above options. What's the worst thing that can happen if you do nothing? That's your call.

D - Harm: Yelling, shaming, bribing them to clean the playroom, punishing them for not cleaning, paying them to do the job.

You may have noticed I included "paying children money to do a job" in the Option D – Harm section. You may be now asking yourself, *But why, Michelle? Is that a typo? Isn't it normal to pay kids to do their chores?*

It may be typical and accepted practice, but it is NOT good parenting.

DO NOT TIE ALLOWANCE TO CHORES AROUND THE HOUSE.

Should I repeat that? Okay, I will then.

DO NOT TIE ALLOWANCE TO CHORES AROUND THE HOUSE.

Why is this?

Children need to contribute at home *because they live there.* They're part of the community of home. They matter. Each person does. And each person can and should contribute to the community of home. Chores are something they should do because they live there. More on this coming up in the next chapter.

When we pay our children for jobs, it initially appears to be quite effective. They're highly motivated to complete the tasks so they can earn the pretty colored paper that has all that power associated to it. And—wait for it—the backfire occurs a week or two later.

YOU: "Jane, I need your help emptying the dishwasher."

JANE: "How. Much. Do. I. Get?"

Your head explodes now. You feel infuriated!

Why is this?

Because you've unwittingly created a "what's in it for me?" mentality. A selfish mentality. By paying them for chores, they now expect it every time you need a hand around the house. You've produced an individualistic perspective, rather than a sense of care and concern for the whole family unit and the needs of that unit.

DO NOT PAY YOUR CHILDREN FOR HOUSEHOLD TASKS. However….

DO PAY THEM!

Just not in exchange for anything. *What is this strange concept, Michelle?*

There's a great reason for giving your children money free and clear of any work they owe you in return. And that reason is to teach them money management. THAT is a necessary life skill. Unfortunately, it's not a class offered in high school. *We* need to teach them. Teach them and let them feel what it's like to save money, spend it, have some to spend, blow it on "plastic fantastics" (those inexpensive toys that often break quickly).

All those things.

That's why they need an allowance—to experiment with money. And to learn how it feels in each of those experiences. You'll be building in them a healthy relationship with money—as a resource and something of value that must be managed.

The best time to start giving allowances to children is around age five. Prior to age five, money is simply pretty paper to them. They don't understand its value. Around age five, they start to understand it wields the power of exchange; they can get things with it! For younger children, you may need to give allowances every week and then older kids can be once a month. When you give them an allowance, start teaching them what they can do with it if they save it, and help them set goals for how they will spend it.

•••

WHEN MY KIDS WERE YOUNGER and wanted to earn extra money, I'd help them brainstorm tasks they could do for the *neighbors* (pick up sticks, rake, weed, etc.) and then I'd prep the neighbor in advance. I'd even offer to *pay them* to pay my child for the job! It was a perfect learning opportunity on how to earn money.

Picking up sticks at *our* house was simply needed and a way for them to contribute to the community of our home…of which they are a part, so I was not comfortable paying them for that.

On good parenting days, I would check in with how they felt about themselves and their job and acknowledge how their participation specifically impacted the whole. "We can play outside now because you picked up the sticks while I did the dishes. Now we have time to swing!" Notice that none of this was bribery *before* the task. It was simply an observation after the fact!

Kids need to have responsibilities at home.

They also need to learn money management.

So, let's not mix up the two.

They can and should be separate life skills…independent of each other.

Stay away from option D and you will be a perfEct parent.

FIFTEEN

Chores at Home: How to Get Them Done Willingly?

Expecting your kids to accomplish *anything* without your participation is setting yourself up for disappointment. Can we just agree on that upfront? One thing is certain—your child has to be *capable* of the tasks you're expecting them to do. So, this discussion isn't really about the younger kids; their attention spans are too short for chores independent of us parents.

This is for the older crowd.

When older kids don't help with chores, what do you do?

How can you get them to participate?

What if you did nothing to intervene? (That is a natural consequence).

Just leave the dirty dishes there. If you're able to do nothing, and not intervene, what would happen to the dishes? They would stay there, right? Does your child EVENTUALLY get around to them?

Short term pain is… looking at dirty dishes and tolerating their presence in the sink that YOU *really* want to be clean and empty. Long term gain is if you are able to stop talking about it and the child actually does the dishes eventually. It just may not always be in our timeframe. If that is the pattern in your house and the child actually DOES get around to doing them, then allow the natural consequence to happen.

Are you able to manage your feelings around that? And let it be? Let go?

I was only able to for so long.

Then we made an agreement. We agreed the dishes were to be done before bed. You may have an agreement with your child that they're to be done immediately following dinner. The agreement has to work for you, in your house.

Not mine.

Not your sister's.

Not your best friend's.

So, have some agreement.

···

WE DID. WE HAD SOME AGREEMENT. And *sometimes* the dishes got done before bed and *sometimes* they didn't get done. It is those times when they didn't get done, and just sat there, stinking and growing, that I plotted in my heart a plan. I mean, what is a sane parent to do?

On more than one occasion, my children have reported that dirty dishes mysteriously appeared in their bathroom sink or on their beds, of all places! How strange.

I'm not proud to report that.

Simply honest.

The dishes, only then, began to inconvenience *them*. Sitting in the kitchen sink, they were inconveniencing *me*. In their beds, they didn't like it so much.

Logical consequences, natural consequences and punishment...what is the difference among those three? And what is a *sane* parent to do?

A *natural consequence* is if we do nothing to intervene and allow the consequence to speak for itself. If the child doesn't eat their dinner, then the natural consequence is that they will be hungry. The natural consequence of not taking a coat to school is that they are cold at recess. For me, a natural consequence of speeding is that I receive a ticket. The natural consequence of not doing your own laundry (older kids included) is that their favorite items are not clean.

I have often been asked, "When can we parents begin to allow natural consequences to happen?" Let's go back to the time your child was in a highchair. Remember how they would take the sippy cup and knowingly drop it over the edge of the tray and watch it land on the floor? And they would do this while smiling at you?

And then, what did you do?

Willingly pick it up? The first time. And what about the second and third times that they did it? Were you getting more and more frustrated?

Me too.

Remember, a natural consequence relieves us of having to intervene.

So, if we do not retrieve the cup off the floor when it is tossed overboard, what does the child learn then?

The very small person in the highchair learns: *if I throw the cup over, it doesn't come back.*

Remember how problems have owners? You picking it up makes it *your* problem. Letting it remain "overboard" makes it *their* problem. They learn that if they want their drink, it needs to stay on the tray. It is a felt experience of learning. And they do learn.

A *logical consequence* has to meet the test of the four R's, according to Kathryn Kvols in *Redirecting Children's Behavior*; otherwise it is a punishment (and they usually hate us for those since they are arbitrary and unrelated to their offense). The 4 R's are:

Is it **r**easonable?

Is it **r**elated to the offense?

Does it teach **r**esponsibility?

Is it **r**espectful?

Was putting the dishes in their bedroom respectful? Not sure about that one.

Reasonable? Yes.

Related to the situation/problem? Yes.

Teach them responsibility? Yes.

There you have it. A logical consequence (for the most part) regarding the dishes.

So, it is up to us to create logical consequences rather than punishments. They are far more effective, and the child feels accountable for the offense and consequence. It is a sense of "I did this to myself" instead of "you did this to me."

How to implement "chores" or "jobs" as a normal practice in your home?

Remember that need for power we all have? The easiest way to give power is to offer choices. Where chores are concerned, allow your children to choose.

Make a list on the computer of the chores that need to be done around the house for a Saturday morning. After each task on the list, type a blank line. Chores like feeding the dog, doing dishes, loading the dishwasher, etc. Those may rotate weekly or monthly or whatever plan works in your home. Make sure you indicate that recurrence on your list.

Our Saturday list had maybe six or seven jobs and a line next to each one where the kids could sign up for that job, writing their name on the blank line. I'd let them know on Saturday morning that the list was out. They would RUN to sign up for the jobs.

Why?

Because they wanted to get the jobs they *preferred*.

We all have preferences.

Some of us *love* to fold clothes, some hate it. Some of us *love* to clean bathrooms, some hate it. Some *love* dishes. Some hate it.

Kids are the same.

[NOTE: The chores list might also list at the bottom the normal daily chores that are *already* assumed for each child in your home—those that don't rotate. Examples of daily assigned chores might include picking up the clothes in each of their rooms, making their bed—if that's a daily thing in your house (it wasn't for me)—putting away clean clothes into their closet or drawers.]

So, we would highlight the jobs on the list that were needed for that Saturday, and the artificial boundary we created was that they needed to be completed BEFORE lunch. If the jobs were not completed before lunch, that meant my child was not ready for lunch.

It happened often.

I found it hard to not coax or remind them, knowing that keeping my mouth shut was the most effective route. If they didn't comply and I said nothing, they would suffer the natural consequences. (Saying nothing to intervene and let the natural consequence happen is THE most effective learning tool.) So, in this case, a few hours later, lunchtime rolls around and it was then that the rubber hit the road. It went like this:

While looking at the list, I asked, "What has been completed?" or "How did picking up the sticks go?" It was obvious who had completed their assignments—we would eat lunch with whomever had finished their jobs. Natural consequences: no lunch until you finish your task.

Lunch continued to be available to all after their jobs were completed.

Consequences.

They work.

And, there was no D. No shame, no yelling, no bribing, no payments.

"Nagging makes it your problem. Silence makes it theirs." ~Barbara Colorosa

Chores at Home: How to get them done willingly? Option A to D

A - Ideal: Be clear what your expectations are regarding the how, when, what of doing dishes or any other chore you want the kids to do in your home. Stop reminding and nagging.

Say it once and follow through a thousand times by not saying anything. Allow the natural consequence to occur if possible. Say nothing until lunchtime or dinnertime (whatever your timeframe for job completion is) and then broach the subject of the chores (even though you have likely observed whether the child has been on task or not). Less is more here.

If they still won't do their chores, give them a logical consequence that aligns with the four "Rs"—Is it reasonable? Related to the offense? Teach responsibility? Is it respectful? For example, if their assigned responsibilities are not complete by the agreed upon timeframe, then a logical consequence might be that they then get to do an additional job for the family. This would be helpful to be communicated at the outset so the child knows the logical consequence ahead of time. If they haven't done the dishes by the time you arrive home, then they agree they will be doing another job, like walking the dog or picking up dog leftovers in the yard!

One client claims that she can make *anything* related to the cellphone so that the phone can be factored into any logical consequence!

B - Good: Do any lighter version of the above.

The logical consequence where the dishes appeared once on their bed and once in their bathroom sink? I wouldn't call that our "parent of the year" consequence. It really might not be an "A," so perhaps it fits here in the "good enough" area...B.

While they're doing the dishes, it can even be a good time to connect with your child about their day. Or your day. If you want your child to converse with you, you also need to share about yourself. Otherwise, it's a one-sided conversation and it can feel a bit like an interrogation. Dialogue involves two. So maybe it can be less painful if there is conversation? You decide. Sometimes it is best to leave them alone. Attitude doing a job is okay (no, it is not ideal). The thing is, we first need for them to be *doing* the job before we can work on the attitude *while* they are doing the job! Always discipline behavior and not attitude.

> Nagging makes it your problem.
> Silence makes it theirs.
> - Barbara Colorosa

C - Do no harm: Say nothing. Let the dishes pile up and see how long it takes for them to get to their task. What's the worst thing that can happen? (Okay, so maybe you *might* want to rinse if bugs are a concern?)

D: Harm: Shaming, bribing, yelling, humiliating, punishing, threatening.

Stay away from option D and you will be a perfEct parent.

SIXTEEN

Letting Others Be the Authority

This one is more about you than about them. Say you've got a child melting down at Target. Or the dentist. Or a restaurant. Or the doctor's office. Or ANYWHERE! You're feeling helpless at the situation as it gets more and more out of control. What do you do?

Relief is at hand! Bet you didn't know you've got a secret weapon in your tool belt—the authorities! Consider using those in charge who surround you. They are there. They're like cops. Lean on them. Engage them in your plot. It's brilliant!

Why do I say that?

You don't have to be the bad guy. Someone else already is.

In Target?

Quietly and privately ask the cashier, manager, or uniformed salesperson to come say a few words to your child about what is expected there. Children have inherent respect for (by that I mean submission to) authority figures who are not their parents. So, use that to your advantage.

For instance, you might have the store manager say, "Please keep your voice down. We have lots of shoppers here and the screaming is hurting their ears."

Or, "We need you to sit down in the cart to be safe as our floors hurt when you fall on them."

What about in a restaurant?

Have the server come over and tell your child that "In our restaurant, we SIT in the chairs." Or, "We talk softly in this restaurant." Or, "We keep our food on our plates here." This message is consistent with the messages *you're* sending. And, these messages have a new gravity/novelty to your child when delivered by someone *else*...especially someone in a uniform or with a nametag! They look official, right?

At the dentist?

Ask the staff (in private) to have a chat about teeth brushing and what *they* expect from your child. What *they* expect in regard to your child's teeth. And maybe ask them to share pictures or information with the child about what happens if they *don't* comply with good oral hygiene. Pictures of what "yuck mouth" actually looks like!

Information is empowering. And sometimes frightening (in a good way).

At our house when there was resistance to teeth brushing, we told our kids, "You only have to brush the ones you want to keep." (Humor helps!) I would try to remove myself from further being Grace's authority by asking her, "What does Dr. Hayes want you to do with your teeth?" Or, "What will you tell her when you go back to see her and she asks you about how you've been treating your teeth?" I would try to keep it between her and the dentist and not insert myself in the middle.

Parents are the first authority for our children. And we have that role for a long, long time. Any time we can recruit others to reinforce the very same messages we deliver OVER AND OVER can have a significant, positive effect on the child. They truly hear it differently from them. They seem to hear it almost as if it's new information!

And, it's a consistent message reinforcing the one *we've* been sending to our kids.

The more of these influences a child hears, the more likely the message will get planted into their little minds.

We are planting seeds. And, we need as many people as we can to water these seeds!

It takes a village.

Then, it is no longer personal. The child (especially teenagers) often hears the opinion of the parent and dismisses it.

In one ear and out the other.

When that very same message is received by the child from *another* authority figure, it carries a different weight.

They hear it in their heads like this: *Maybe my dad isn't so crazy. Dr. Hayes wants me to do the same thing.* Or, *Okay, so the other people in the restaurant don't want me bouncing around this booth either.*

They feel the gravity of the message.

It's received differently—with more weight.

We do the same thing. We may hear one message about health and dismiss it. Then, we may keep getting that same message and begin to pay more attention to it. Or we hear it from someone else whom we respect.

Resistance is human nature. We're working with what we got!

•••

I REMEMBER ONE NIGHT TRYING TO CONVINCE Grace to take this horrible-tasting medicine she was required by our pediatrician to take. Remember, this is the child, in regard to food, who could "taste it with her eyes"? I really felt bad for her having to take this awful stuff, but I knew she needed to take it. I couldn't get her to do it.

On a good night, her resistance was naturally high! So I used the doctor's authority and let her take on the role of cop.

"What would Dr. Renbarger say about not taking the medicine? What do you think will happen to your body if you don't take it?" I asked Grace.

My question made her think about the longer term results of not taking it, and not just about the moment. I made her consider something bigger than just right now and the yucky taste of the medicine.

Kids are reasonable people. And, information is empowering.

So are authority figures.

Enroll them.

Enroll them often!

Save yourself by having them reinforce your very same message.

And, that child of mine with the VERY sensitive taste buds? Her finely tuned superpowers of taste and smell? She is now an adult. I've encouraged her to consider becoming a sommelier in her spare time or a perfumier in Paris. The world needs noses and taste buds like hers. She can detect the subtlest notes of flavors and scents. She still has that superpower as an adult!

How sharing an "I" message in Target changed the kids perspective

An **"I" message** has four parts to it.

I feel _____(name the feeling that you are experiencing)

When _____(state whatever it is that is occurring WITHOUT using the word "YOU" since that word will make them defensive as it is the verbal version of pointing our finger at someone.

Because _____(what is the value or why is this important for you?)

"What I would like" or "would you please"? _____
_____(ask for what you want and if possible offer a choice for them that meets the need of power.)

When we own our feelings, it makes the other person, or child, more open and less defensive in the situation. And, we usually don't do an "I" message naturally. Usually, we deliver a more targeted statement that makes the other person defensive.

So, in Target, the problem is that we want and need our child to stay in the same aisle as us so we can see them. We want and need them to stay near us. Our verbal delivery of this need usually sounds something like this: "Get over here! Get in the cart! Stay in this aisle!"

Notice that each of those are commands. And, as humans, we ALL (adults and children) resist commands. Nobody likes being told what to do. Our children included.

When I finally remembered the "I" message as one of the tools in my toolbox, this is what came out. And it changed all future trips to Target and the grocery.

"Grace,

I feel *scared*

When I cannot see my kids in the same aisle as me

Because it is my job as your mom to take care of you and keep you safe

So, would you please stay in the same aisle where I can see you and you can see me? Or stay in the cart?

Everything changed after that.

I could see the compassion in their eyes when I delivered that message. I could see that it softened them. They had empathy for me knowing I was scared and simply trying to do my job. My kids did not want to scare me. And, they understood I was trying to *care* for them and not *control* them.

You see, problems have owners. And, when we deliver the first commanding message to our kids about what they are doing wrong and we are telling them what to do, we are making it their problem and trying to control them.

And, when we state the problem in the form of an "I" message, we are owning the problem. Which is where it belongs. It is our problem. And it is a more honest way to communicate. Owning that which is ours.

"I" MESSAGES

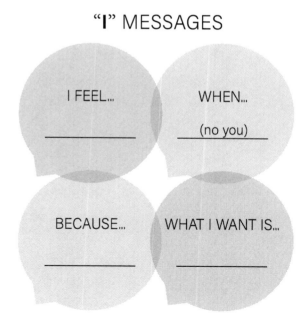

I FEEL...

WHEN...

(no you)

BECAUSE...

WHAT I WANT IS...

A similar message was delivered to Charlie many years later in the teen years regarding curfew. The problem was timeliness of his arrival safely home and what would happen to my thoughts whenever he was five minutes late. They went to dark scary places. And, when our minds create dark, scary pictures we typically project that out in anger with a version of:

"YOU ARE PAST YOUR CURFEW! YOU ARE SO DISRESPECTFUL! (Notice the "you's" and the shaming). And, then we often start spewing the punishments that are going to come hailing down:

"I am going to take away your car and your phone until you honor your curfew!"

Remembering the **"I" message**, this is what I delivered:
"Charlie,

I feel *scared*

When I have not seen or heard from my kids by the time the curfew hour rolls around

Because I start to create scary thoughts of bad things happening to either of you

So, what I would like is to hear from you if you are going to be any minute late after your curfew so that my mind does not go to dark scary places.

That same look of compassion washed over his face.
He ALWAYS let me know.
Without exception.
I received a text or a call sharing with me what was happening.
I owned the problem. It was my problem, after all. My mind created the scary scenes. Not his. This was not his problem what

my mind did. It was mine. And I shared it in this magic way that helped him understand. "I" messages rock. Feel free to use them with your kids, your partner, and at work. They work.

How to Use Authority Figures to Influence Your Kids, Option A to D

A - Ideal: Recruit. Recruit. Recruit.

Recruit any and all uniformed, identifiable authority figures nearby to deliver your child a message similar to the one you've been trying to send. It takes a village! Use them to your advantage as often as possible.

Use **"I" messages** to deliver how you *feel* and what you want. It helps keep the child open to hearing about *your* problem. It is a problem YOU have that clearly is not a problem for them. Delivering it in this format reduces defensiveness. Consider using "I" messages with your partner and at work!

I feel *overwhelmed and distracted*

When I am in staff meetings and taking notes

Because I am trying to listen and write at the same time

What I would like is for one person to capture the notes from the meeting and share them with the group.

"I" messages feel so much kinder to deliver and so much kinder to receive than complaints or attacks.

All that we need to be in this life is reachable and teachable. When we are, we learn and grow.

We can do hard things.

B - Good: If the authority figure isn't in the same proximity to you, verbally remind your child about the authority figures and what they *might* say to your child if they were here, without actually having the real-life exchange. Real life experience is much more impactful if it's possible. But when it isn't, you can still give your child a felt sense of them and their authority on the subject.

C - Do no harm: Same as above.

D - Harm: Encouraging any authority figure to embarrass, shame, humiliate your child. That is NOT the message here. It's simply to deliver information in a respectful, neutral way. A message that reinforces the one you've likely been delivering over and over and over is what we're going for—not negativity!

Simply Stay Away from Option D and you are the perfEct parent.

You got this!

AFTERWORD

"Do Your Best"

Do. Your. Best. It is a line that comes out of every parent's mouth.

"Just do your best."

"Did you do your best?"

"All we want is for you to do your best."

Sounds innocent enough right? Our intentions are good (as they usually are).

It is not innocent.

Allow me to explain…

When you get up in the morning, do you make the best breakfast? Do your hair the best? Exercise the best? Wear the best outfit? Drive the best? Do your best job with your kids? Do your best job at work? Make the best dinner? And on and on it goes.

The problem with this message is that kids know what their best is. Just as we do. And, it changes moment to moment, day to day.

•••

CHARLIE WAS AGE 7 IN SECOND GRADE. He came home and declared, "Mom, I am the fourth smartest in my class." He knew who was getting higher grades on academic work than him. He knew exactly. So, if I were the parent at home telling him, "you are the best student", "you are the best in math/science/spelling/ reading", I lose credibility in doing so. He already knew the hierarchy. He would not believe me intuitively since he already has a gauge there of knowing.

So, what are we to do with this common message? The one that we say internally to ourselves and the one that we deliver verbally to our kids?

Let's get honest. And real. Similar to the option A through D concept.

Consider encouraging your kids to save their "best" efforts on spelling to be for the test on Friday. The pretests are practice. Recognize that and allow space for real, practicing, and growth. Our best and their best may be Option C… do no harm. It may be option B… a 6/10.

In regards to cleaning the room, "just do your best". The range of numbers helped at our house. A version of this was communicated, "I don't need the room to be a 10. I need the stuff on the floor picked up and put away and the bed made." (Specific). Or, "grandma is coming to stay in your room and we need to shoot for a 10 on the job this time" (kind of like the spelling test on Friday).

There are times that we can and need to do our best.

And that is not *every* day in *every* task.

We need not expect it from our kids either. When we do this, it can trigger shame in our kids. It triggers the sense of "not good enough".

They KNOW what their best is and when they give it.

We KNOW what our best is and when we give it.

So, give yourself grace as you consider applying the strategies in this book. Sometimes your "best" will be option C. Same with your sweet kids.

Do no harm.

It could be the very best we have.

And when you have option A in you? Give that. We know that that is not every day all day long.

And neither is it for our kids.

You rock. Your kids need you. Not at your best. Not at their best.

They just need you.

You got this.

About the Author

Michelle Gambs is a parent coach and psychotherapist with a degree from The University of Notre Dame. She has had the concept of this book in her for over ten years and is happy to finally share it. She has seen how the A to D philosophy has relieved her clients through the years. Their shoulders drop. And, they feel permission to be human...knowing that what they are doing with their kids is sometimes stellar (option A), sometimes good enough (option B), and sometimes exiting stage left (option C) is the best they got.

She hosted the podcast ParentED, shares tips on YouTube (bloopers included), offers an online four-week course Redirecting Children's Behavior, and loves coaching parents.

Grace and Charlie continue to give her opportunities to grow on this journey of life and parenting. It remains the role in her life that has been the most rewarding and the most challenging. During the most desperate stages of parenting, she posted on her bathroom mirror the quote, "I never said it would be easy, I only said it would be worth it."

Find Michelle at:
MichelleGambs.com
stayawayfromoptiond.com
Instagram: @michellegambs
Facebook.com/michellegambs
YouTube: Michelle Gambs

Made in the USA
Columbia, SC
31 March 2021